MW01028271

INVESTIGATING THE
BOOK OF MORMON
WITNESSES

INVESTIGATING THE BOOK OF MORMON WITNESSES

RICHARD LLOYD ANDERSON

Deseret Book Company
Salt Lake City, Utah

Cover photos Church Archives, The Church of Jesus Christ of Latter-day Saints

© 1981 Deseret Book Company

All rights reserved. No part of this book may be reproduced in any form or by any means without permission in writing from the publisher, Deseret Book Company, P. O. Box 30178, Salt Lake City, Utah 84130. This work is not an official publication of The Church of Jesus Christ of Latter-day Saints. The views expressed herein are the responsibility of the author and do not necessarily represent the position of the Church or of Deseret Book Company.

DESERET BOOK is a registered trademark of Deseret Book Company.

Visit us at DeseretBook.com

First printing in hardbound, 1981
First printing in paperbound, 1989

Library of Congress Cataloging-in-Publication Data

Anderson, Richard Lloyd.
   Investigating the Book of Mormon witnesses.

   Includes bibliographical references and index.
   1. Book of Mormon—Evidences, authority, etc.
I. Title.
BX8627.A67   289.3'22   80-26626
ISBN-10: 0-87747-846-5 (hardbound)
ISBN-10: 0-87579-242-1 (paperbound)
ISBN-13: 978-0-87579-242-2 (paperbound)

Printed in the United States of America
Brigham Young University Press, Provo, UT

10   9   8   7   6   5   4   3   2   1

To my children,
Roselle,
Nathan,
Gerrit,
Chandelle,
who were uncomplaining
while their father
gathered information.

Contents

List of Illustrations

Preface

"Let him see anything he wants." This terse response of the LDS Church historian authorized serious research on the Book of Mormon witnesses. At that time I was aware that eleven men had given impressive testimonials in printed and unprinted sources. I was determined to examine original manuscripts and then follow their careers in civil records and newspapers of each county where they lived. Much later I published ten articles (in the *Improvement Era* during the year beginning August 1968) that were valued for their new data by the Mormon History Association, winning the annual award for best article. These installments are updated and presented here with supplementary chapters. In the future I hope to add longer books on the subject, but not more significant ones. Surveys often lightly skim the surface, but a good summary has a far more serious goal. It resembles good art in the sense that it comes only after an author pays the price to know his subject.

Much has been learned about the major Book of Mormon witnesses. Above all is the drama of their solemn affirmations, in the quiet intimacy of friendship and in the hostility of ridicule and even persecution. Theirs is a compelling life story. Here are modern men who can be examined closely on their astounding claim—of being commissioned by an angel's appearance and by God's voice to testify of ancient scripture. Here are others who describe a physical experience of seeing and handling the metal record. Discovery of early scrolls or plates will always fascinate people, and adding the miraculous should only heighten the significance of the claim. Can it be taken seriously? It must be taken seriously if the witnesses' words are taken seriously. These eleven were interviewed by both the careful and the careless, leaving scores of accounts that can furnish not only the accurate quotation, but also the partial quotation and the misquotation. So their true experience will be understood only from their personal writings, speeches, and responsibly reported interviews. These Book of Mormon witnesses sincerely sought answers and risked comfort and honor in unwavering assurance that God had acted. After years of working with their lives and their words, I am deeply convinced that their printed testimonies must be taken at face value.

Acknowledgments

Naming some contributing to this work means that many others go unmentioned because of short space. I owe a debt to the pioneer researchers on the witnesses, Andrew Jenson, B. H. Roberts, and Preston Nibley, and to three whose masters' theses at Brigham Young University were the first systematic collections on the lives of the three witnesses. These men are Wayne C. Gunnell; Ebbie L. V. Richardson; and Stanley R. Gunn, whose work on Oliver Cowdery was published.

The richest resources on the Book of Mormon witnesses are in the archives of The Church of Jesus Christ of Latter-day Saints. Administrators in the Historical Department have given consistent cooperation, including Earl E. Olson, Donald T. Schmidt, Jeffery Johnson, James L. Kimball, Jr., and their competent assistants, who deserve much more than my anonymous thanks here.

Many important manuscripts are at the Library-Archives of the Reorganized Church of Jesus Christ of Latter Day Saints at Independence, Missouri. These were made available over the years by Church Historian Richard P. Howard and many capable assistants. Invaluable help for reconstructing the early community life of the Whitmers was given by friend and local historian John S. Genung of Waterloo, New York. Other essential aid came as publisher John Van Camp allowed me to work evenings and early mornings in the files of the *Advertiser-Tribune* at Tiffin, Ohio, the home of Oliver Cowdery for seven years.

Capable secretaries transformed cluttered drafts into readable pages; they will know the value of their contribution without my making a long list. Some photographs appear by courtesy of the LDS Historical Department or the LDS Graphics Design and Resources Division. My thanks go to *Church News* editor Dell Van Orden for furnishing his photograph of the recently reconstructed Whitmer cabin. Special appreciation goes to my wife, Carma de Jong Anderson, who prepared final copy and did the layout of the Book of Mormon translation map. I continue to benefit from her good judgment in studying early Mormonism, where her interests are as intense as my own.

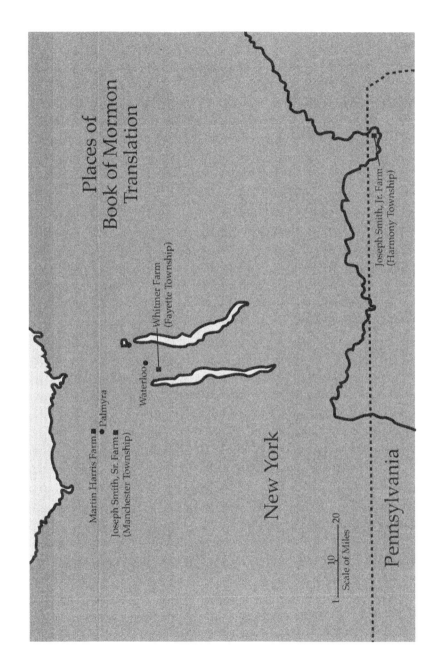

Places of
Book of Mormon
Translation

Martin Harris Farm ■   ● Palmyra

Joseph Smith, Sr. Farm ■
(Manchester Township)

Waterloo ●

Whitmer Farm
(Fayette Township)

New York

Joseph Smith, Jr. Farm
(Harmony Township)

Pennsylvania

1 ⊢—10—⊣—20
Scale of Miles

Whitmer farm and reconstructed family home, Fayette, New York

1

Assistants and Eyewitnesses

Joseph Smith's criticisms of Christianity in the nineteenth century are remarkably like Christian self-criticisms of the twentieth. The youth was confused by multiplying churches and conflicting claims. Christian leaders in recent decades have also repeated their frustration at "the scandal of the divided church." After long inquiry young Joseph found no answers among quarreling leaders, so he turned to God alone. In past decades world councils and international committees have also sought the "renewal of the spirit." But the results are less than convincing. Creeds have softened, inter-faith negotiations continue, but competitive Christianity remains. Its tragedy is the confusion of human systems that inadequately direct the faith of innumerable men and women of great commitment. Early Christians were "of one heart and of one soul" (Acts 4:32), but Christianity now better resembles the early world confounded after Babylonian pride "that they may not understand one another's speech." (Gen. 11:7.) Religious leaders can quote past prophets, but who can divinely lead God's people out of the bondage of confusion today?

1

This question is even more urgent than it was on the spring day of 1820 when Joseph Smith strode into the New York woods and returned shaken by a divine decree: "I was answered that I must join none of them, for they were all wrong."[1] This message may be ridiculed or ignored, but precedents are on Joseph Smith's side, for few religious systems have escaped the gradual corruption of embracing the world that they originally were called to confront. What have past prophets said as they returned from sacred visions? Isaiah was overwhelmed by God's presence and received the message that his generation no longer knew God—that they would hear "but understand not," that they would see "but perceive not." (Isa. 6:9.) Six centuries later Jesus quoted these words to the Jewish people in solemn warning that they no longer walked in God's path. (Matt. 13:14–15.) Ezekiel also withstood the glory of the Lord and received from his lips the commission to go to the chosen but "rebellious nation"—for "they and their fathers have transgressed against me, even unto this very day." (Ezek. 2:3.) Ezekiel then tasted the book of God's decree for the Israelites, sweet because it came from the Lord and bitter because it condemned their sins and promised judgment. Nor did the God who called the early Christians speak with another voice. Six decades after the crucifixion John the Revelator came from the fiery vision of the exalted Christ to severely warn the Christian churches that they would lose their places without immediate repentance. (Rev. 2:5.) Who has aspired to God's presence today? The blunt condemnation of current religions reported by Joseph Smith is a profound mark of credibility when read by the light of past prophets.

Measuring a prophet is not unlike other serious decisions of life. Mosaic law required solid proof: "at the mouth of two witnesses, or at the mouth of three witnesses, shall the matter be established." (Deut. 19:15.) Prophets independently substantiate other prophets. Even Jesus had the comfort and strength of the testimony of John the Baptist, to whom he referred as a second witness on more than one occasion. (Matt. 11, John 5:33.) And nothing is more dominant in the early chapters of Acts than the force of many witnesses, the united testimony of apostles who had seen the resurrection for themselves. The public ministry of the latter-day Prophet also involved his associates as witnesses. The three called to tell of the angel and the plates were vital personalities of historical interest in their own right. But their story is really part of the larger story of the unfolding revelations to their leader—the call to restore ancient scriptures and reestablish Christ's Church with authority.

The Book of Mormon witnesses testified of the truth of an ancient book, but its significance can only be seen by the meaning of events that brought them together in the new cause of God. As Luke said in reviewing earliest Christianity, the founding events rest on reports of those who "from the beginning were eyewitnesses." (Luke 1:2.) First there were Joseph's visions, and afterward men were called to verify their reality. This story of the sharing of the burden will later be told through the eyes of each witness, for each reiterated his printed testimony and also verified many surrounding experiences that remained inspirational for a lifetime. Full information on how the Book of Mormon witnesses were called is found in the straightforward recollections of founder Joseph Smith, supplemented by those of his mother. These two are important "eyewitnesses," so their narratives will appear below with minimal explanations. An outline of these beginning events is in an appendix at the back of this book for easy reference.

Since the adult Joseph Smith was a prayerful man, he is all the more convincing in relating his 1820 prayer concerning which church was right. His first letter to his wife comes a dozen years later and speaks of time spent while waiting for the opportunity to return to her: "I have visited a grove which is just back of the town almost every day, where I can be secluded from the eyes of any mortal and there give vent to all the feeling of my heart in meditation and prayer."[2] This is the language of practiced communion with God. The 1820 petition was answered with the command not to join established churches—to "continue as I was until further directed."[3] That direction came as he neared his eighteenth birthday. The radiance of God's glory is the most striking first impression of the visions of Isaiah, Ezekiel, and John mentioned above. The same brilliance filled the many divine visions of Joseph Smith in the 1820 decade. On the night of September 21, 1823 he prayed intensely to know God's further will toward him. Steadily the soft darkness about him was transformed into blinding brilliance. Oliver Cowdery privately talked with Joseph Smith about the experience and reported: "Indeed, to use his own description, the first sight was as though the house was filled with consuming and unquenchable fire."[4] No wonder the Prophet's earliest picture of the glorious messenger comes in similar terms: "an holy angel, whose countenance was as lightning and whose garments were pure and white above all whiteness."[5]

The angel was Joseph's teacher—that night; the next morning at the hill, where he was instructed to wait until further maturity; and periodically during the next four years before getting the plates before dawn on September 22, 1823. In midcareer the Prophet concisely summarized how he obtained the Book of Mormon: "Moroni, the person who deposited the plates from whence the Book of Mormon was translated, in a hill in Manchester, Ontario County, New York, being dead and raised again therefrom, appeared unto me and told me where they were and gave me directions how to obtain them. I obtained them and the Urim and Thummim with them, by the means of which I translated the plates. And thus came the Book of Mormon."[6]

As he prepared for translation, Joseph grew to young manhood. One month after he turned twenty-one, he married Emma Hale, his intensely religious and intelligent companion. A rural schoolteacher of considerable native talents, Emma gave Joseph her deepest loyalty, which strongly suggests total sincerity in his religious life. These young adults married over the objections of Emma's father and therefore lived in their first year with Joseph's parents on their New York farm a few miles from where the plates were buried. That fall they went together to the hill, where Emma waited while Joseph received the inscribed record of an ancient American civilization and its prophets. The angel instructed Joseph again on obedience, promising divine protection in the coming attempts to steal the plates and to frustrate his work of translation. The next chapter will re-create these first trials through the recollections of Joseph's immediate family.

Martin Harris and his wife were the first beyond Joseph's family to be interested in the new work. Joseph correctly called him "a farmer of respectability,"[7] and he could have had little interest in young Joseph Smith, poor son of a struggling farmer, except for a deep conviction of the truth of Joseph's confidential story of being called to translate an ancient record that he had newly acquired. Joseph's mother tells how Martin had just arranged his affairs for a year's vacation for travel, providentially allowing time to help Joseph in the translation during the summer of 1828. Before that took place, however, community rumors incited jealousy, resulting in several attempts to take the plates. So for safety Joseph and Emma moved near her father's farm in Harmony township, Pennsylvania, where the couple managed thirteen acres and settled in their own small house. By this time Martin

Harris was convinced enough to hand Joseph fifty dollars in moving expenses in public, at the same time commenting, "I give this to you to do the Lord's work with; no, I give it to the Lord for his own work."[8]

This local aristocrat was now the most active adherent of the Prophet. Soon after Joseph and Emma returned to Pennsylvania, Martin traveled over a hundred miles to obtain characters copied from the plates and then continued his winter journey another hundred miles to New York City. There he called on linguists, including the learned Columbia classics professor Charles Anthon. Some details of the Harris-Anthon conversation are unclear, but Martin was convinced all of his life that the professor had fulfilled Isaiah's prophecy of a learned man getting "the words of a book that is sealed," being asked to read, and responding, "I cannot; for it is sealed." (Isa. 29:11.) Anthon confirmed this much in two later letters on the subject, insisting that the characters presented to him were unintelligible, as indeed they should have been, since Egyptian had not been deciphered in his day, nor have many other near-eastern and middle-American scripts. Joseph Smith's earliest private understanding of what Harris said is in his first biography, written in 1832. He wrote that Martin came to Pennsylvania, where Joseph had recently moved with the plates, "and said the Lord had shown him that he [Martin] must go to New York City with some of the characters, so we proceeded to copy some of them, and he took his journey to the eastern cities and to the learned, saying, Read this, I pray thee, and the learned said, I cannot, but if he would bring the plates they would read it."[9]

Martin Harris would later finance the first printing of the Book of Mormon, but his considerable role in the beginning translation is now apparent, followed by two intensive months as Joseph Smith's scribe in the summer of 1828. Their work produced 116 manuscript pages, which were entrusted to Martin on his pleading for evidence to soften his critical household. Joseph imposed strict conditions, which Martin Harris did not keep. Since his carelessness made possible the loss of the manuscript, Martin was rebuked in further revelations, directing Joseph not to use this man again as secretary, but to wait for further assistance. Nevertheless, Martin Harris continued his intense interest in the translation in the face of the fury of his wife, and he later pledged valuable land against the printing costs for the Book of Mormon some weeks after seeing the angel and the plates.

The translation lagged in the winter after the loss of the 116 pages. Practical work for survival drained the strength of Joseph and Emma, who sometimes helped as a secretary then. But this discouraging winter season at the Prophet's home in Harmony was also the time of conversion for Oliver Cowdery at the Prophet's parents' home in Manchester, where he boarded as district schoolteacher. Convinced that God had called him to assist, he arrived to write for the Prophet in early April, 1829, and the efficient team had apparently finished the major segments of the ancient record when they moved to Fayette, New York two months later. By then they had also received together personal visits of New Testament prophets and apostles, restoring authority to baptize and direct Christ's church. No one exceeded Oliver Cowdery in contributions of time or effective talent to this daily work of restoration. Nearly ninety percent of the surviving pages of original dictation are in his handwriting.[10]

By this time Joseph and at least one secretary knew that there would be witnesses of the plates, for there was a revelation on this subject just before Oliver Cowdery arrived to help. Martin Harris again had traveled to Harmony to satisfy recurring doubts about the plates. The words of inspiration came to assure that three would see the plates, and that if faithful, he would be one of the three. The general promise of this event was clear: "Yea, and the testimony of three of my servants shall go forth with my words unto this generation. Yea, three shall know of a surety that these things are true, for I will give them power, that they may behold and view these things as they are, and to none else will I grant this power to receive this same testimony among this generation."[11]

This promise given in Pennsylvania would be fulfilled in New York, for Joseph Smith and Oliver Cowdery would move in midtranslation because of threats of violence. Oliver explained these in a letter to his friend David Whitmer, who then prayed to know whether he should bring the translators to his father's New York home. The whole Whitmer family weighed the request and became convinced that God had called them to his work. So David made the sacrifice to travel to Pennsylvania and get the translators. As this expanded household gathered socially in the evenings, there were obviously times of reading the manuscript and discussing its exciting truths. In this setting came a "discovery" that there would be three witnesses, though clearly a rediscovery for Joseph Smith and Martin Harris, who shared in the above revelation March, 1829. Sometime in May the new scribe, Oliver Cowdery, had perhaps recorded one of two Book of Mormon prophecies on witnesses.[12] Then during June the translation continued after the move to Fayette, where the "discovery" of the witnesses prophecy took place as the translation was nearing its end. From the Prophet's language, the following promise seems the one that intensified the desires of his associates to become witnesses:

Wherefore at that day when the book shall be delivered unto the man of whom I have spoken, the book shall be hid from the eyes of the world, that the eyes of none shall behold it save it be that three witnesses shall behold it, by the power of God, besides him to whom the book shall be delivered; and they shall testify to the truth of the book and the things therein.

And there is none other which shall view it, save it be a few according to the will of God, to bear testimony of his word unto the children of men; for the Lord God hath said that the words of the faithful should speak as if it were from the dead.

Wherefore, the Lord God will proceed to bring forth the words of the book; and in the mouth of as many witnesses as seemeth him good will he establish his word; and wo be unto him that rejecteth the word of God.[13]

In mentioning Book of Mormon promises, the Prophet depicts the deep desires of three whose contributions to the translation had been most critical. With this work nearly over, both Book of Mormon prophecies concerning witnesses were probably known—and the one not quoted above named the witnesses as "those who shall assist to bring forth this work." (Ether 5:2.) That verse aside, it was still inevitable that those who were doing the most to produce the book had the greatest emotional interest in seeing the treasured plates that it came from. That interest had earlier caused Martin Harris to ask Joseph and to get the inspired promise of "a view of the things which he desireth to know," on condition that he would "humble himself in mighty prayer and faith."[14] Just in their capacities as secretaries, Martin Harris and Oliver Cowdery had contributed far more personal time than anyone else. And although several Whitmer brothers had been equally zealous, David Whitmer's help had been critical because of the timing of moving the translators when their work would otherwise have stopped. Thus with strong reasons for their expectations to be witnesses, they approached the Prophet:

In the course of the work of translation we ascertained that three special witnesses were to be provided by the Lord, to whom he would grant
that they should see the plates from which this work (the Book of Mormon)

should be translated, and that these witnesses should bear record of the same . . .

Almost immediately after we had made this discovery, it occurred to Oliver Cowdery, David Whitmer, and the aforementioned Martin Harris (who had come to inquire after our progress in the work) that they would have me inquire of the Lord, to know if they might not obtain of him to be these three special witnesses. And finally they became so very solicitous, and teased me so much, that at length I complied, and through the Urim and Thummim, I obtained of the Lord for them the following revelation: . . . [15]

As the prophet indicates, this inquiry of the three was answered by an affirmative revelation. Their faith was evidently great, for the promises were great, not only to see the plates, but also the sacred relics that had been hidden up by the early American prophets. Those who see the witnesses as victims of simple deception have overlooked the complexity of the experience promised to them, and their later spontaneous mention of seeing the other ancient objects with the plates:

Behold I say unto you, that you must rely upon my word, which if you do with full purpose of heart, you shall have a view of the plates, and also the breastplate, the sword of Laban, and Urim and Thummim, which were given to the brother of Jared upon the mount, when he talked with the Lord face to face, and the miraculous directors which were given to Lehi while in the wilderness on the borders of the Red Sea. And it is by your faith that you shall obtain a view of them, even by that faith which was had by the prophets of old.

And after that you have obtained faith, and have seen them with your eyes, you shall testify of them by the power of God. And this you shall do that my servant Joseph Smith, Jr., may not be destroyed, that I may bring about my righteous purposes unto the children of men in this work.[16]

All of the foregoing discussion has set the stage for the striking experiences reported in simplicity by the witnesses themselves and by Joseph Smith, who shared the vision of the

Three Witnesses and who accompanied the Eight Witnesses to the grove where they lifted and examined the plates. Conventional writing detracts from the powerful realities reported by these participants. Only through their words can we appreciate what happened. The Prophet's mother adds great insight into the surrounding circumstances, though careful readers must be cautious enough to realize that her recollections are partial glimpses, not total inventories. The following sources are the vivid narratives of what was seen and physically sensed by all twelve witnesses, including Joseph Smith. The importance of their reports is highlighted here by reproducing their words without comment. These narratives begin with Lucy Smith taking the reader into the Whitmer home as the translation was being finished.

Preparations of the Three Witnesses

"Here they continued translating until the whole work was completed. They then lost no time in informing us—that is, his father's family—of the accomplishment of this very important duty. We communicated this intelligence to Martin Harris the same evening, for we loved the man, although his weakness had cost us much unnecessary trouble. He seemed to have a heart that designed no evil, and we felt a commiseration for the disappointment which he had brought upon himself in an evil hour. When he heard that the translation was finally completed, he seemed as greatly rejoiced as if he knew that it had affected his salvation, and determined to go straightway to Waterloo as soon as he could get away the next morning. We accordingly set off together, and before sunset we met Joseph and Oliver at Waterloo. The evening was spent in reading the manuscript, and it would be superfluous for me to say to anyone who has read these pages that we were greatly rejoiced, for it then appeared to us who did not realize the magnitude of the work, which could hardly be said at that time to have beginning, as though the greatest difficulty was then surmounted. But with Joseph it was not so, for he knew that a dispensation of the gospel was committed to him, of which the starting bud had scarcely yet made its appearance.

"The next morning after breakfast was over, we repaired to the sitting room, and after attending the morning service Joseph approached Martin with a solemnity which I thrill through my veins to this day whenever it comes to my recollection. 'Martin Harris,' said he, '*you* have got to humble yourself before your God this day and obtain if possible a forgiveness of your sins. And if you will do this, it is his will that you and Oliver Cowdery and David Whitmer should look upon the plates.' Soon after this these four left and went into a grove a short distance from the house." (Lucy Smith, preliminary manuscript of *Biographical Sketches,* also cit. *Biographical Sketches,* pp. 138–39.)[17]

The Angel and Plates: Joseph Smith's Testimony

"Not many days after the above commandment was given, we four—viz., Martin Harris, David Whitmer, Oliver Cowdery and myself—agreed to retire into the woods, and try to obtain by fervent and humble prayer the fulfilment of the promises given in the revelation that they should have a view of the plates, etc. We accordingly made choice of a piece of woods convenient to Mr. Whitmer's house, to which we retired. And having knelt down we began to pray in much faith to Almighty God to bestow upon us a realization of these promises. According to previous arrangements I commenced by vocal prayer to our heavenly Father, and was followed by each of the rest in succession. We did not yet however obtain any answer or manifestation of the divine favor in our behalf.

We again observed the same order of prayer, each calling on, and praying fervently to God in rotation, but with the same result as before. Upon this our second failure, Martin Harris proposed that he would withdraw himself from us, believing as he expressed himself that his presence was the cause of our not obtaining what we wished for.

"He accordingly withdrew from us, and we knelt down again and had not been many minutes engaged in prayer when presently we beheld a light above us in the air of exceeding brightness. And behold, an angel stood before us. In his hands he held the plates which we had been praying for these to have a view of. He turned over the leaves one by one, so that we could see them, and discover the engravings thereon distinctly. He addressed himself to David Whitmer, and said, 'David, blessed is the Lord, and he that keeps his commandments.' When immediately afterwards, we heard a voice from out of the bright light above us, saying: 'These plates have been revealed by the power of God, and they have been translated by the power of God. The translation of them which you have seen is correct, and I command you to bear record of what you now see and hear.'

"I now left David and Oliver, and went in pursuit of Martin Harris, whom I found at a considerable distance, fervently engaged in prayer. He soon told me, however, that he had not yet prevailed with the Lord, and earnestly requested me to join him in prayer that he also might realize the same blessings which we had just received. We accordingly joined in prayer, and ultimately obtained our desires, for before we had yet finished, the same vision was opened to our view—at least it was again to me. And I once more beheld, and heard the same things, whilst at the same moment, Martin Harris cried out, apparently in ecstacy of joy, 'Tis enough; mine eyes have beheld,' and jumping up he shouted, hosannah, blessing God, and otherwise rejoiced exceedingly." (Joseph Smith,

13

History of the Church 1:54–55, in the form first published in *Times and Seasons* 3 [1842]:897–98.)

Return of the Three Witnesses

"They returned to the house. It was between three and four o'clock. Mrs. Whitmer and Mr. Smith and myself were sitting in a bedroom. I sat on the bedside. When Joseph came in he threw himself down beside me: 'Father! Mother!' said he, 'you do not know how happy I am. The Lord has caused the plates to be shown to three more besides me, who have also seen an angel and will have to testify to the truth of what I have said. For they know for themselves that I do not go about to deceive the people. And I do feel as though I was relieved of a dreadful burden, which was almost too much for me to endure. But they will now have to bear a part, and it does rejoice my soul that I am not any longer to be entirely alone in the world.' Martin Harris then came in. He seemed almost overcome with excess of joy. He then testified to what he had seen and heard, as did also others, Oliver and David. Their testimony was the same in substance as that contained in the Book of Mormon. . . .

"Martin Harris particularly seemed altogether unable to give vent to his feelings in words. He said, 'I have now seen an angel from heaven, who has of a surety testified of the truth of all that I have heard concerning the record, and my eyes have beheld him. I have also looked upon the plates and handled them with my hands and can testify of the same to the whole world. But I have received for myself a witness that words cannot express, that no tongue can describe, and I bless God in the sincerity of my soul that he has condescended to make me—even me—a witness of the greatness of his work and designs in behalf [of] the children of men.' Oliver and David also joined with him in solemn praises to God for his goodness and mercy." (Lucy Smith, preliminary manuscript of *Biographical Sketches*, also cit. *Biographical Sketches*, p. 139.)

Writing the Testimony of Three Witnesses

"Having thus through the mercy of God, obtained these manifestations, it now remained for these three individuals to fulfil the commandment which they had received, viz., to bear record of these things, in order to accomplish which, they drew up and subscribed the following document:" (Joseph Smith, *History of the Church* 1:56, in the form first published in *Times and Seasons* 3 [1842]:898.)

The Testimony of Three Witnesses

"Be it known unto all nations, kindreds, tongues, and people, unto whom this work shall come, that we, through the grace of God the Father, and our Lord Jesus Christ, have seen the plates which contain this record, which is a record of the people of Nephi, and also of the Lamanites, his brethren, and also of the people of Jared, which came from the tower of which hath been spoken; and we also know that they have been translated by the gift and power of God, for his voice hath declared it unto us; wherefore we know of a surety, that the work is true. And we also testify that we have seen the engravings which are upon the plates; and they have been shewn unto us by the power of God, and not of man. And we declare with words of soberness, that an Angel of God came down from heaven, and he brought and laid before our eyes, that we beheld and saw the plates, and the engravings thereon; and we know that it is by the grace of God the Father, and our Lord Jesus Christ, that we beheld and bear record that these things are true; and it is marvellous in our eyes.

Nevertheless, the voice of the Lord commanded us that we should bear record of it; wherefore, to be obedient unto the commandments of God, we bear testimony of these things. And we know that if we are faithful in Christ, we shall rid our garments of the blood of all men, and be found spotless before the judgement seat of Christ, and shall dwell with him eternally in the heavens. And the honor be to the Father, and to the Son, and to the Holy Ghost, which is one God. Amen."

> OLIVER COWDERY
> DAVID WHITMER
> MARTIN HARRIS
> (Copy of the three witnesses' testimony from the 1830 edition of the Book of Mormon.)

Background on the Eight Witnesses

"We returned home the next day, a cheerful, rejoicing little company. In a few days we were followed by Joseph and Oliver and the Whitmers, who came to make us a visit and also to make some arrangements about getting the book printed. Soon after they came, they all—that is the male part of the company—repaired to a little grove where it was customary for the family to offer up their secret prayers. Joseph had been instructed that the plates would be carried there by one of the ancient Nephites. Here it was that those eight witnesses recorded in the Book of Mormon looked upon the plates and handled them." (Lucy Smith, preliminary manuscript of *Biographical Sketches*, also cit. *Biographical Sketches*, p. 140.)

"Soon after these things had transpired, the following additional testimony was obtained:" (Joseph Smith, *History of the Church* 1:57, *Times and Seasons* 3 [1842]:898.)

The Testimony of Eight Witnesses

"Be it known unto all nations, kindreds, tongues, and people, unto whom this work shall come, that Joseph Smith, Jr. the Author and Proprietor of this work, has shewn unto us the plates of which hath been spoken, which have the appearance of gold; and as many of the leaves as the said Smith has translated, we did handle with our hands; and we also saw the engravings thereon, all of which has the appearance of ancient work, and of curious workmanship. And this we bear record, with words of soberness, that the said Smith has shewn unto us, for we have seen and hefted, and know of a surety, that the said Smith has got the plates of which we have spoken. And we give our names unto the world, to witness unto the world that which we have seen: and we lie not, God bearing witness of it."

> CHRISTIAN WHITMER
> JACOB WHITMER
> PETER WHITMER, Jr.
> JOHN WHITMER
> HIRAM PAGE
> JOSEPH SMITH, Sen.
> HYRUM SMITH
> SAMUEL H. SMITH
> (Copy of the eight witnesses' testimony from the 1830 edition of the Book of Mormon.)

Joseph Smith on the Plates and "Interpreters"

"These records were engraven on plates which had the appearance of gold. Each plate was six inches wide and eight inches long, and not quite so thick as common tin. They were filled with engravings in Egyptian characters, and bound

17

together in a volume as the leaves of a book with three rings running through the whole. The volume was something near six inches in thickness, a part of which was sealed. The characters on the unsealed part were small, and beautifully engraved. The whole book exhibited many marks of antiquity in its construction, and much skill in the art of engraving. With the records was found a curious instrument, which the ancients called 'Urim and Thummim,' which consisted of two transparent stones set in the rim of a bow, fastened to a breast plate. Through the medium of the Urim and Thummim I translated the record by the gift and power of God." (Joseph Smith, "Wentworth Letter," *Times and Seasons* 3 [1842]:707, also *History of the Church* 4:537.)

Recalling the Book of Mormon Revelations

"And again, what do we hear? Glad tidings from Cumorah! Moroni, an angel from heaven, declaring the fulfilment of the prophets—the book to be revealed. A voice of the Lord in the wilderness of Fayette, Seneca County, declaring the Three Witnesses to bear record of the book." (Beginning of Joseph Smith's list of early revelations, letter to the Church, Sept. 6, 1842, first published in *Times and Seasons* 3 [1842]: 935–36, now D&C 128:20.)

NOTES

1. Joseph Smith, *History of the Church* 1:6, also Pearl of Great Price, JS-H 1:19, reprinted also in the LDS pamphlet "Joseph Smith's Testimony."

2. Joseph Smith to Emma Smith, June 6, 1832, Greenville, Indiana, manuscript at the Chicago Historical Society.

3. HC 1:8, JS-H 1:26.

4. *Latter Day Saints' Messenger and Advocate* 1 (1835):79.

5. "Articles and Covenants of the Church of Christ," first published in *The Evening and the Morning Star,* June, 1832, now D&C 20:6.

6. *Elders' Journal,* July, 1838, pp. 42–43.

7. HC 1:19, JS-H 1:61.

8. *Biographical Sketches,* p. 113.

9. See Joseph Smith, 1832 Manuscript History, in Dean C. Jessee, ed., *The Personal Writings of Joseph Smith* (Salt Lake City: Deseret Book, 1984), pp. 7–8. The second Anthon Transcript and the apparent Joseph Smith note on it, pp. 223–26 of this book, proved to be forged.

10. See the valuable tabulation of surviving pages of the original Book of Mormon manuscript in Dean C. Jessee, "The Original Book of Mormon Manuscript," *Brigham Young University Studies* 10 (1970):273.

11. Book of Commandments 4:4, the earliest datable writing (1833), with subsequent verbal changes in D&C 5:11–14. An undated manuscript of the early form is in the Whitney papers at Brigham Young University, box 1, folder 2.

12. Cowdery's priesthood restoration narrative indicates that by May 15, 1829, the translators had passed 3 Nephi 11, which raises the authority question that caused their inquiries on baptism. See *Latter Day Saints' Messenger and Advocate* 1 (1834):13: "after writing the account given of the Savior's ministry." The next book, Ether, 5:24 contains the promise of witnesses seeing the plates.

13. In the next quotation of the text, the Prophet mentions the Book of Mormon promise in language much closer to this 2 Nephi 27 prophecy than to Ether 5:2–4, which suggests that they were in Fayette translating the first two books of Nephi, the period of the lost 116 pages. The non-Cowdery manuscript pages, some of which are apparently done by John Whitmer, also indicate a Fayette translation for the beginning portions of the book. Cp. n. 10.

14. Book of Commandments 4:8, with the Whitney manuscript reading "the things which he desireth to view," now D&C 5:24. Cp. n. 11.

15. *Times and Seasons* 3 (1842):897, also cit. HC 1:52–53.

16. D&C 17:1–4, first published in the 1835 edition with the dating: "June, 1829, given previous to their viewing the plates containing the Book of Mormon." Early dissenter Ezra Booth saw a manuscript of this revelation in the summer of 1831: "When in Missouri, I had an opportunity to examine a commandment given to these witnesses, previous to their seeing the plates. They were informed that they should see and hear those things by faith and then they should testify to the world." (Letter 3, [Ravenna] *Ohio Star*, Oct. 27, 1831.)

17. Joseph Smith's history suggests that Book of Mormon translation was nearly completed at this time, a correction of Lucy Smith, who did not live in the Whitmer home but only visited. In Lucy's manuscript at the end of the quotation here, "four" is written over an original "three," referring to those who then left the home. Since David remembered being in the field when others came to get him, he may not have been at the morning devotional service. There are other possibilities of time, since we have only glimpses of that morning in the sources.

William Smith (1811–93)
Younger brother of Joseph Smith, Jr.

2

Informal Witnesses
of the Plates

Reality is greater than short official statements. The testimony of the Three and Eight Witnesses is a bold design in a whole pattern of events. The official witnesses gave their names to two documents that outlined their experiences in seeing the plates in June, 1829. Yet the plates figured in the regular life of Joseph Smith for over a year and a half prior to that. He worried about obtaining them, guarded them carefully during this period, and used them in translation for many months. This meant that those nearest him shared in his strategies for preserving and using them. So a larger circle than the official witnesses had some contact with the ancient record in their daily affairs. The plates were brought to Father Smith's home in Manchester, New York; then taken to the Prophet's home in Harmony, Pennsylvania; after which they were transported to Father Whitmer's home in Fayette, New York, to finish the translation. Most of the Smith and Whitmer men became formal witnesses of the plates. But what did the women and older children of these households say, including the Prophet's wife?

Joseph went to the Hill Cumorah late on the night of September 21, 1827 and some time after midnight obtained the plates.[1] But his mother makes clear that he did not bring the ancient book home then. Instead he found a decayed tree in the woods for a hiding place, and returned to bring the plates to his house about a day and a half later. Mother Lucy Smith's history gives the fullest details of this night: Joseph's going alone to the forest cache about three miles from his house and scraping away the covering bark from the records, after which he "took them from their secret place, and wrapping them in his linen frock, placed them under his arm and started for home."[2] But Joseph was assaulted several times as he cut through the woods to avoid traveled places. Alternately fending off his attackers and outrunning them, he threw himself breathless in a fence corner "in sight of the house." His mother adds, "And as soon as he could go on he rose and finished his race for the house, where he arrived altogether speechless from fright and exhaustion."[3]

Besides Joseph there were six children then living in the home. Samuel later joined married brother Hyrum to give his name publicly as a witness. William became the most articulate spokesman for the rest, partly because he lived until 1893 and was sought out for his recollections. In his eighty-two-year life span he was outspoken on his early experiences in the Smith family. When Joseph first brought in the plates, William was an impressionable sixteen-year-old, of large build and aggressive. Joseph's overgarment made of tow, or rough-woven linen, figures prominently in William's recollections, as it does in Lucy Smith's history. The following is part of a speech of William, his most detailed picture of Joseph's entering the home with the ancient record.

When the plates were brought in they were wrapped up in a tow frock. My father then put them into a pillow case. Father said, "What, Joseph, can we not see them?" "No. I was disobedient the first time, but I intend to be faithful this time. For I was forbidden to show them until they are translated, but you can feel them." We handled them and could tell what they were. They were not quite as large as this Bible. Could tell whether they were round or square. Could raise the leaves this way (raising a few leaves of the Bible before him). One could easily tell that they were not a stone, hewn out to deceive, or even a block of wood. Being a mixture of gold and copper, they were much heavier than stone, and very much heavier than wood.[4]

Joseph's father was not allowed to see the plates then, but he became an official witness. This was after the translation was finished, as William explained to an educated minister who reported his conversation in 1841: Joseph Smith "kept the plates a long time in his chamber, and after translating from them, he repeatedly showed them to his parents and to other friends. But my informant said he had never seen them."[5] But picking them up and feeling their contour was another matter, for at the end of the above speech William was asked how much the plates weighed, and his answer was: "As near as I could tell, about sixty pounds."[6] William said the same thing in the early story of Mormonism that he authored, recounting how Joseph "escaped to the house and brought the plates with him—wrapped up in a towfrock."[7] In the same work William sharply distinguished himself from his father and brothers Hyrum and Samuel, "who were witnesses to the truth of the book."[8] They had this additional privilege later, for William could say of himself (and the family) on the night that Joseph brought in the plates: "I was permitted to lift them as they laid in a pillowcase, but not to see them, as it was contrary to the commands he had received. They weighed about 60 lbs. according to the best of my judgment."[9] All of William's reports of lifting and feeling seem to refer to this same night, for Joseph did not usually keep the plates wrapped in his work smock, which William called "his everyday frock such as young men used to wear then."[10] Not long before his death, William reiterated his vivid experience with the plates to interviewer J. W. Peterson. "Bro. Briggs then handed me a pencil and asked Bro. Smith if he ever saw the plates his brother had had, from which the Book of Mormon was translated. He replied, 'I did not see them uncovered, but I handled them and hefted them while wrapped in a tow frock and judged them to have weighed about sixty pounds. I could tell they were plates of some kind and that they were fastened together by rings running through the back.' "[11]

Mother Lucy Smith shared William's experiences, but she also had some others. Her son Joseph showed her both the Urim and Thummim and the breastplate, the objects obtained in the box with the plates, apparently to ease her worries and reward her for her intense concern about obtaining the plates.[12] Her view of these things may account for the above minister's report from William that Joseph had showed the plates to his parents; in fact only the father saw the plates, but perhaps William hinted that his mother had seen things not shown to him. As far as the ancient records, Lucy is like William, for both said that they had not seen but had picked them up. This new information from Lucy is not from her dictated memoirs, but from an 1838 letter from a neighbor, a convert who wrote her relatives in response to their request for something to strengthen their faith after the difficult financial troubles and apostasy in Kirtland. The author of the following letter had temporarily moved back to her mid-Ohio home but reviewed her close association with the Prophet's mother, telling the same stories that Lucy Smith later put in her memoirs about hiding the plates from neighbors who sought to take them. Since these are events of October and November, 1827, a period of about eight weeks, the "eight months" of the following report may be miswritten. Otherwise this letter summarizes well the events of the Smith family in these two months with the same intimate details that are only found in Lucy Smith's history.

> I lived by his mother, and [she] was one of the finest of women—always helping them that stood in need. She told me the whole story. The plates was in the house and sometimes in the woods for eight months on account of people trying to get them. They had to hide them. Once they hid them under the hearth. They took up the brick and put them in and put the bricks back. The old lady told me this herself with tears in her eyes, and they ran down her cheeks too. She put her hand upon her stomach and said she [ha]s the peace of God that rested upon us, all that time. She said it was a heaven below. I asked her if she saw the plates. She said no, it was not for her to see them, but she hefted and handled them, and I believed all she said, for I lived by her eight months, and she was one of the best of women.[13]

Such a record of a woman's private conversation is all too rare in history, but there is every reason to suppose that Joseph Smith's sisters could have told equivalent stories. Of course, youngest sister Lucy was only six when Joseph brought home the plates and probably said little about it; similar considerations may have influenced youngest brother Don Carlos, then eleven, though also pertinent is his early death at the age of twenty-five in Nauvoo. The two sisters nearer Joseph's age were modest people and evidently did not talk much about their experiences. Yet their overall faith in their brother's mission supports their sharing the events mentioned by William and mother Lucy Smith. For instance, a Mormon elder saw the sisters Sophronia and Katharine in 1856 and reported after a long visit, "They testified that they knew that their brother Joseph was a Prophet of God."[14] Their special family knowledge was earlier tested by Martin Harris, for he told how careful he had been in investigating the Book of Mormon soon after Joseph got the plates. He first allowed his wife and daughter to visit the Smith house and afterwards questioned them about the box that supposedly held the plates. "My daughter said they were about as much as she could lift . . . and my wife said they were very heavy." Martin Harris decided to see for himself and while there also lifted the box of plates. "I knew from the heft that they were lead or gold, and I knew that Joseph had not credit enough to buy so much lead."[15] All of this fits the Lucy and William recollections, but the point here is Martin Harris's individualized cross-examination of "Joseph, his wife, brothers, sisters, his father and mother. I talked with them separately, that I might get the truth of the matter." In fact, Martin arrived on the above visit when Joseph was away. "I was glad he was absent, for that gave me an opportunity of talking with his wife and the family about the plates. I talked with them separately, to see if their stories agreed, and I found they did agree."[16]

Joseph's younger sister Katharine was no doubt in the house at this time. When Joseph got the plates she was fifteen, and she also summarized the events of that night, though what stands out is her disappointment at Joseph's not fully sharing the plates. "We had supposed that when he should bring them home, the whole family would be allowed to see them, but he said it was forbidden of the Lord. They could be seen only by those who were chosen to bear their testimony to the world. We had therefore to be content until they were translated and we could have the book to read. Many times when I have read its sacred pages, I have wept like a child, while the Spirit has borne witness with my spirit to its truth."[17] Katharine Smith Salisbury lived longest of all of the immediate family of the Prophet, but up to her death in 1900 was not interviewed systematically. Yet her educated grandson, Herbert S. Salisbury, reported her private conversations about Joseph's first bringing the plates home. "She said he entered the house running and threw himself on a couch, panting from his extraordinary exertion. She told me Joseph allowed her to 'heft' the package but not to see the gold plates, as the angel had forbidden him to show them at that period. She said they were very heavy."[18]

Joseph had received the plates late in September, 1827, and in the following weeks endured constant harassment from excited neighbors determined to get them. Mother Smith told not only of hiding them under the hearth, but also of having a mob ransack their cooper's shed and smash apart the box that the plates had been removed from.[19] When Joseph moved to Pennsylvania in December, another group conspired to waylay him, but broke up arguing with each other.[20] Finally Emma and Joseph arrived at her father's farm, where they settled on a small acreage and fixed up a house for their needs. In the spring of 1828 Martin Harris came some 130 miles from their former home to live with Joseph and Emma and spend his time writing manuscript while Joseph dictated the translation. By mid-June Emma was ready to deliver her first child, and the men were at a stopping point in their work. Double sorrow now descended on Joseph and his wife. Against divine direction, Joseph had taken the responsibility of loaning the manuscript to Martin Harris for the purpose of convincing his hypercritical wife and certain friends. Soon after Harris left, Emma's child came but died right after birth.[21] Then Emma's life hung in the balance for a time, but as she recovered, she was as worried about the manuscript as Joseph was, and urged him to go to Palmyra to find out why Martin had sent no word. Under great physical hardship Joseph did this, only to find the worst—Martin had been careless, and the manuscript had disappeared. Joseph detailed in his history how he was rebuked, stripped of both plates and translating aids for a time, and that fall reintrusted with the commission to translate the Book of Mormon. But Martin Harris, who had violated his solemn commitments, was not again allowed to write for the work. Joseph said that during that fall and winter he marked time, devoting himself to farming for a living, but in his early summary history he added of this winter of 1828–29: "now my wife had written some for me to translate, and also my Brother Samuel H. Smith."[22] This knowledge gives great value to his wife's candid comments on the translation process.

The Prophet's problem of how to proceed was moving to solution in his parent's home that winter. Oliver Cowdery had been engaged as the schoolteacher in that district and boarded at the Smiths. Fascinated by the rumors he had heard regarding the finding of the ancient record, Oliver carefully investigated the facts from Joseph's parents, who shared their knowledge fully with him as they learned to trust him. Through prayer he received confirmation of Joseph's mission, and traveled 130 miles to help with the translation in Pennsylvania in early April, 1829.[23] For the next two months Oliver boarded with Joseph and Emma and wrote as the religious record of ancient American peoples was deciphered. This period of the translation at Emma's home in Harmony, Pennsylvania, offered her additional opportunity to observe. Here Joseph's wife had cooked and cleaned for the translating team for two months during 1828 and now again for two months during 1829, doubling as secretary herself during several months between these periods. All of this was in a small house with few rooms. No doubt her comments are most significant.

Emma outlived Joseph by a third of a century and had strong opinions on the inspired nature of Book of Mormon translation. Her overall impression is clear: "And though I was . . . present during the translation of the plates, and had cognisance of things as they transpired, it is marvelous to me, 'a marvel and a wonder,' as much so as to any one else."[24] She stressed that Joseph worked beyond his natural abilities that she well knew, not relying on any English aid or even mental review to create the narrative. Right after talking with his mother, Joseph III reported her responses in a letter. "She wrote for Joseph Smith during the work of translation, as did also Reuben Hale, her brother, and O. Cowdery; that the larger part of this labor was done in her presence, and where she could see and know what was being done; that during no part of it did Joseph Smith have any mss. or book of any kind from which to read, or dictate, except the metallic plates, which she knew he had."[25]

How did she know that Joseph had the plates? In the same interview Emma described how she would write for him "day after day, often sitting at the table close by him." He would translate by excluding the light from his interpreting stone by a hat. Some have assumed that this process went on without the plates, since Emma said that he sat at this table "dictating hour after hour with nothing between us."[26] But the plates evidently had a constant function in their work, since they were also at the same table. The question was asked about her husband, "Are you sure that he had the plates at the time you were writing for him?" This was Emma's full answer: "The plates often lay on the table without any attempt at concealment, wrapped in a small linen table cloth, which I had given him to fold them in. I once felt of the plates as they thus lay on the table, tracing their outline and shape. They seemed to be pliable like thick paper, and would rustle with a metallic sound when the edges were moved by the thumb, as one does sometimes thumb the edges of a book."[27] Emma made clear that she did not attempt to remove the cover from the plates, though she was certain what they were. "I moved them from place to place on the table, as it was necessary in doing my work."[28]

Emma's quiet valley was finally infested with ugly threats of persecution as the translation progressed in late spring of

1829. At that point Oliver wrote his acquaintance David Whitmer, who in company with his unmarried brothers worked with Father Whitmer on their farm near Seneca Lake, back in western New York some thirty miles from Palmyra. David Whitmer lived long and was interviewed enough to leave detailed recollections of the events that followed Cowdery's request for help. His father doubted whether he should take six days for the round trip to Pennsylvania at the critical season of spring planting. But the whole household was humbled by clear evidences of divine help, and David set out with team and wagon, bringing Joseph Smith and Oliver Cowdery to his rural Fayette home, leaving Emma to settle up business and follow later.[29] In later life David relived the journey, picturing himself and Oliver on the spring seat of the wagon, with Joseph behind on the board bed. The earliest journal account relates David's story as follows: "And an aged man about 5 feet 10, heavy set and on his back an old fashioned army knapsack strapped over his shoulders and something square in it, and he walked alongside of the wagon and wiped the sweat off his face, smiling very pleasant. David asked him to ride and he replied, 'I am going across to the Hill Cumorah.' Soon after they passed, they felt strange and stopped but could see nothing of him—all around was clear. And they asked the Lord about it. He said that the Prophet looked as white as a sheet and said that it was one of the Nephites, and that he had the plates "[30] In another interview David portrayed the messenger carrying the plates, "about 5 feet 8 or 9 inches tall and heavy set," with "large" face, "a suit of brown woolen clothes, his hair and beard . . . white."[31]

After the translators had moved into the Whitmer home, Mother Whitmer told David a remarkable episode of the same messenger. "My mother was going to milk the cows, when she was met out near the yard by the same old man (judging by her description of him) who said to her: 'You have been very faithful and diligent in your labors, but you are tried because of the increase of your toil; it is proper therefore that you should receive a witness that your faith may be strengthened.' Thereupon he showed her the plates."[32] David gave other details to Edward Stevenson. "She said that they were fastened with rings, thus: $\text{\textcircled{=)}}$. He turned the leaves over; this was a satisfaction to her."[33] She also added of the plates "that a portion of them were sealed together."[34] In telling the story David alluded to the large Whitmer family and the added burden of "Joseph, his wife Emma, and Oliver." Thus the special manifestation had the compassionate purpose of comforting the woman in the household who shouldered the most cares in the new translation arrangement. David said: "And although she had never complained, she had sometimes felt that her labor was too much, or at least she was perhaps beginning to feel so. This circumstance, however, completely removed all such feelings and nerved her up for her increased responsibilities."[35]

David told the above details after his mother's death. Then soon after David's death Mormon historians visited his nephew, John C. Whitmer, a grandson of Mary Musselman Whitmer through her son Jacob. He reiterated the above experience of Mother Whitmer, but with fascinating supplementary details that deserve to be repeated in his own words. He insisted that he had heard the story independently from Mary herself. "I have heard my grandmother say on several occasions that she was shown the plates of the Book of Mormon by an holy angel, whom she always called Brother Nephi." This account was printed by LDS historian Andrew Jenson a month after he had interviewed Mother Whitmer's grandson.

One evening, when (after having done her usual day's work in the house) she went to the barn to milk the cows, she met a stranger carrying something on his back that looked like a knapsack. At first she was a little afraid of him, but when he spoke to her in a kind, friendly tone, and began to explain to her the nature of the work which was going on in her house, she was filled with unexpressible joy and satisfaction. He then untied his knapsack and showed her a bundle of plates, which in size and appearance corresponded with the description subsequently given by the witnesses to the Book of Mormon. This strange person turned the leaves of the book of plates over, leaf after leaf, and also showed her the engravings upon them; after which he told her to be patient and faithful in bearing her burden a little longer, promising that if she would do so, she should be blessed and her reward would be sure, if she proved faithful to the end. The personage then suddenly vanished with the plates, and where he went, she could not tell. From that moment my grandmother was enabled to perform her house-hold duties with comparative ease, and she felt no more inclination to murmur because her lot was hard. I knew my grandmother to be a good, noble and truthful woman, and I have not the least doubt of her statement in regard to seeing the plates being strictly true. She was a strong believer in the Book of Mormon until the day of her death.[36]

The Book of Mormon translation was largely finished at the Whitmer home in Fayette, New York, during June, 1829, the same month in which the Three and the Eight Witnesses saw the plates. These two events gave impressive evidence of the sacred record that Joseph Smith translated, though they are also a part of the larger picture of many people concerned with the translation. The others had knowledge of the ancient record virtually in proportion to their sacrifices to help in translation. Joseph's brother William, his mother Lucy, and his wife Emma all gave early recorded statements of lifting and feeling the original record. And Mary Whitmer's special view was relayed later through the responsible words of her son and grandson. These experiences are not part of the formal proclamation to the world. They are a treasure of personal knowledge that was quietly shared, not to plead a case but to relate why the Book of Mormon touched each life profoundly. These private encounters with the metal book preceded both the Three Witnesses' seeing the angel and the plates, and also the Eight Witnesses' handling the plates in natural surroundings. The final events climaxed household events in which the plates played a part. Thus family knowledge solidly supports the public statements of the Three and Eight Witnesses.

NOTES

1. Lucy Smith, *Biographical Sketches,* pp. 99–101, narrates that Joseph and Emma left about midnight of September 21, but did not return until early morning of September 22, the date which Joseph gives for getting the plates in *History of the Church* 1:18.

2. *Biographical Sketches,* p. 104.

3. Lucy Smith, manuscript of *Biographical Sketches.* See also *Biographical Sketches,* p. 105.

4. William Smith, "Sermon in the Saints' Chapel," Deloit, Iowa, June 8, 1884, *Saints' Herald* 31 (1884):643–44.

5. James Murdock to the *Hartford Observer,* June 19, 1841, New Haven, Conn., *Peoria* (Ill.) *Register,* Sept. 3, 1841.

6. William Smith, Sermon, p. 644.

7. William Smith, *William Smith on Mormonism* (Lamoni, Iowa, 1883), p. 11.

8. Ibid., p. 12.

9. Ibid.

10. Interview of William Smith with E. C. Briggs and J. W. Peterson, *Zion's Ensign,* Jan. 13, 1894, p. 6.

11. Ibid.

12. See *Biographical Sketches,* pp. 101, 107.

13. Sally Parker to Francis Tufts, Aug. 26, 1838, evidently written at Sunbury, Ohio, and posted at Kirtland Mills. Manuscript in possession of a descendant.

14. G.F.A. Spiller to T.B.H. Stenhouse, Dec. 8, 1856, Saint Louis, cit. *The Mormon,* Dec. 20, 1856. Cp. Richard Lloyd Anderson, "What Were Joseph Smith's Sisters Like?" *Ensign,* Mar., 1979, pp. 42–44.

15. Joel Tiffany, "Mormonism—No. II," *Tiffany's Monthly* 4 (1859):168–70 Martin Harris seems responsibly reported by Tiffany, with the exception of the discovery of the plates, where Tiffany admits that he is interested in proving Mormonism a product of superstition or spiritualistic influence. Not only does the Tiffany interview show serious inconsistency on this issue, but reading of all of his installments on Mormonism discloses that he as an interviewer was highly interested in using Harris to support his preconceived explanations.

16. Ibid., pp. 167, 169.

17. Katharine Salisbury letter, Mar. 10, 1886, Fountain Green Township, Ill., cit. *Saints' Herald* 33 (1886):260. First name spelling follows this printed letter and other similar signatures of this period.

18. The quotation comes from Salisbury's most reliable document, his signed typescript, "Things the Prophet's Sister Told Me," June 30, 1945.

19. See *Biographical Sketches*, pp. 108–9.

20. For the date of the move and a summary of persecution, see HC 1:18–19. For aborted plans to take the plates as Joseph was moving, see *Biographical Sketches*, p. 113.

21. HC 1:20–21 gives the approximate translation dates of April 2 to June 14, 1828. For the family tragedy that accompanied the loss of the 116 pages, see *Biographical Sketches*, pp. 118–22, which is confirmed by the death date of the first son on the gravestone: June 15, 1828.

22. HC 1:28 gives a one-sentence summary of Joseph's practical affairs that winter, but his 1832 ledger book manuscript mentions the limited translation: "History of the Life of Joseph Smith, Jr.," p. 6. Cp. Lucy's report of Joseph's conversation this winter; "I have again commenced translating, and Emma writes for me." *Biographical Sketches*, p. 126.

23. For events mentioned, see *Biographical Sketches*, pp. 128–31. Both Joseph and Oliver gave his arrival as April 5, 1829, with translation beginning immediately afterward. HC 1:32 and *Latter Day Saints' Messenger and Advocate* 1 (1834):14.

24. Emma Smith, Interview between Feb. 4 and Feb. 10, 1879, *Saints' Herald* 26 (1879):290.

25. Joseph Smith III to James T. Cobb, Feb. 14, 1879, Letterbook 2, pp. 85–88, RLDS Archives, courteously shared with me by Smith family scholar Buddy Youngreen.

26. *Saints' Herald* 26 (1879):289.

27. Ibid., p. 290.

28. Ibid.

29. The Whitmer family reactions are told by Lucy Smith, who knew the parents well. *Biographical Sketches*, pp. 135–37. For further detail see Richard L. Anderson, "The Whitmers: A Family That Nourished the Church," *Ensign*, Aug., 1979, p. 36.

30. Edward Stevenson, Journal, Dec. 23, 1877.

31. Orson Pratt and Joseph F. Smith to John Taylor, cit. *Deseret News*, Nov. 16, 1878.

32. Ibid.

33. Stevenson, Journal, Dec. 23, 1877.

34. Stevenson, Journal, Feb. 9, 1886. Stevenson also noted David's retelling the same incident in the journal entry of January 1, 1887, recording another visit.

35. Pratt and Smith to Taylor, cit. *Deseret News*, Nov. 16, 1878.

36. Andrew Jenson, *The Historical Record*, Oct., 1881, p. 621. Edward Stevenson was also present at the visit with John C. Whitmer and approved Jenson's report. See Edward Stevenson, "The Thirteenth Witness to the Plates of the Book of Mormon," *Juvenile Instructor* 24 (1889):23.

R. JOHNSON

LAW NOTICE.

COWDERY & WILSON, Attorneys and Counselors at Law, and Solicitors in Chancery, will attend to business entrusted to their management in the several courts in this State, and in the Circuit and District courts of the United States. Office in the Grand Jury room.

Tiffin, Ohio, June 2, 1843.—6m

Refer to
His Excellency, W. Shannon, Columbus, O.
    Hon. John Brough,   "
    Gen. H. A. Moore,   "
    S. Medary, Esq.   "
    Hon. R. Wood, Cleveland.
    Payne & Wilson,   "
    Hon. B. Bissel, Painesvile.
    "   B. B. Taylor, Newark.
    "   E. Lane, Norwalk.
    "   M. Birchard, Warren.
    "   N. C. Read, Cincinnati.
    "   R. P. Spalding,   "
    "   Van R. Humphrey, Hudson.
    Parrish & Snow, Esqrs. Canton.

FOR SALE.

SEVERAL NEW and SUPERIOR WAGONS for sale. Also, one large Penn-

Law card of Oliver Cowdery and partner, 1843
Printed in the Seneca Advertiser, Tiffin, Ohio.

3

Oliver Cowdery:
Non-Mormon Lawyer

Oliver Cowdery played an extraordinary role in the beginning of The Church of Jesus Christ of Latter-day Saints. His title of "second elder" was appropriate, as an examination of incidents in which he was prominent indicates: the translation of the Book of Mormon, restoration of the Aaronic and Melchizedek priesthoods, printing of the Book of Mormon, the conversion of Sidney Rigdon, and the vision of the Christ and the Old Testament prophets in the Kirtland Temple. Since he was announced as the sole companion of Joseph Smith in the foundation experiences, no one else stood in the unique position of being able to expose Joseph Smith at all critical points, if he could be exposed. Because whatever Oliver Cowdery reported about the earliest events of Mormonism is of the greatest significance, it is most important to study the kind of man he was and assess his reliability.

Oliver Cowdery was respected by associates wherever he lived. The pinnacle of his Latter-day Saint career was in Kirtland, Ohio, in 1836, when he was a trusted "assistant president" to Joseph Smith and was involved on many practical fronts of the expanding LDS movement.[1] In that year he reassumed the editorship of the Church newspaper, and his brother-in-law characterized him publicly as "a man of piety, of candor, of truth, of integrity, of feeling for the welfare of the human family, and in short, he is a man of God."[2]

Although Cowdery was prominent in Ohio, the history of Mormonism in Missouri is written with his name largely in footnotes. Personally hurt in his relationship with Joseph Smith, he allied himself with his Whitmer relatives in serious differences with the Church as it was gathering in Caldwell County, Missouri. The Whitmers were in local leadership and also involved in land promotion that might be considered either private enterprise or—as was interpreted by Missouri members—the exploitation of the Saints. Oliver sided with this family as he attempted to build up his personal fortune through beginning legal work. Six of nine charges against him involved his economic affairs, and his part in filing collection suits was specifically named. This Book of Mormon witness penned a spirited letter of resignation, in which he defined his controversy with leaders not in terms of basic beliefs, but only "the outward government of this Church."[3] He left Missouri after mob violence and by the end of that year found his way back to Ohio. In the decade between his excommunication from the Church in 1838 and his return in 1848, his name is absent from Mormon activity.

But no one can make an intelligent appraisal of Cowdery as a person without knowing a good deal about his non-Mormon career. By failing to conform to Church discipline, he forfeited his title of "second elder" and exchanged it for "Oliver Cowdery, Esquire," the traditional designation of an attorney-at-law. Without companionship of his Church associates, he nevertheless belonged to the fraternity of fellow attorneys, who admired him as a legal craftsman. During his non-Mormon decade, he was also a politician, journalist, promoter of education, and civic servant. The opinions of his friends of this period show clearly that he was widely respected as a man of more than ordinary stature.

By the time of his excommunication on April 12, 1838, Oliver Cowdery had made definite plans for the practice of law. The only question was where. He exchanged much correspondence with his brothers in Kirtland in hopes of settling in the same vicinity, and one letter states his ideal of professional competence:

"I take no satisfaction in thinking of practicing law with a half dozen books. Let us get where people live, with a splendid library, attend strictly to our books and practice, and I have no fear if life and health are spared, but we can do as well as, at least, the middle class."[4]

After experimenting with living in Missouri, he decided to move back to Ohio, where his brothers Warren and Lyman were beginning their careers in the field of law. This move to Kirtland took place at the end of 1838, and by January 1840 it is clear that Oliver Cowdery was practicing law.[5] The year 1839 was undoubtedly devoted to study for his admission to the bar,[6] but there were other activities. His biography in the family history was compiled with access to information from his widow, Elizabeth Whitmer Cowdery, who lived until 1892, and it says that he "supported himself by teaching school while pursuing his study of the law."[7] If this phrasing is strictly correct, then Cowdery taught during his non-Mormon stay in Kirtland. Perhaps this is why he appears as secretary of one of the organizational meetings of the Western Reserve Teacher's Seminary and Kirtland Institute, which used the Kirtland Temple in the period that he was there.[8]

Be that as it may, Cowdery was active in the Democratic Party during his Kirtland stay. In 1839 he was chosen as one of the thirteen delegates from Geauga county to the bi-county senatorial convention.[9] The upset victory there for Benjamin Bissell is most interesting,[10] since, as Joseph Smith's attorney at Kirtland, Bissell was well acquainted with Mormon leaders. He is spoken of as Cowdery's patron in introducing him to law, and consequently he was the likely source of Cowdery's recommendation to the Democratic leaders in Tiffin, Ohio, where Cowdery next moved.

The spirited presidential campaign of 1840 necessitated a Democratic paper in Seneca County, Ohio, and both a press and an editor were imported. Cowdery was chosen for that job, obviously on the basis of recommendations of prominent Democrats of his Cleveland-Kirtland region, some 125 miles northeast. A prominent Tiffin politician later said of the founding of that campaign paper, "Oliver Cowdery was to have been editor, but was dropped on the discovery that he was one of the seven founders of Mormonism."[11] If the arithmetic of the six organizers or the eleven witnesses is garbled, the recollection is clear that a Book of Mormon witness was no political asset and could not be tolerated in a local party post. The fact that Oliver Cowdery nevertheless remained in Tiffin for seven years and earned the respect of a biased community says a good deal for his personal capacities and character. Before leaving he was appointed temporary editor of the Democratic weekly and was publicly thanked in its columns for his "ability" as shown in "the management of our paper."[12]

While the above incident illustrates Cowdery's lifelong talent as a writer, it was through his profession as a lawyer and his public activities that he was chiefly known while in Tiffin from 1840 to 1847. The courthouse today holds files of legal pleadings signed "O. Cowdery"; the two local newspapers of the period contain both his lawyer's advertisements and the notices of his cases requiring publication. More significantly, two colleagues of that period are on record with their estimate of the man and his legal talent.

William Lang had the greater personal contact with Cowdery, because he apprenticed in his office for the period of one and a half years. Lang was a self-reliant man of twenty-five at the beginning of his period of reading law in the Cowdery office, and the senior attorney created a powerful impression upon his student. This relationship with Cowdery terminated in 1842 upon Lang's own entrance to the bar, but he associated with Cowdery for another five years, both as a member of the Seneca County Bar and in the inner circles of the county Democratic organization. Lang's lifetime legal career was supplemented with public service as prosecuting attorney, probate judge, mayor of Tiffin, county treasurer, and two terms in the Ohio senate. He was nominated by his party for major state offices twice. In later life he wrote a *History of Seneca County,* in which he expressed unlimited admiration for the "noble and true manhood" of Oliver Cowdery. He there describes Cowdery personally and professionally:

> Mr. Cowdery was an able lawyer and a great advocate. His manners were easy and gentlemanly; he was polite, dignified, yet courteous. He had an open countenance, high forehead, dark brown eye, Roman nose, clenched lips and prominent lower jaw. He shaved smooth and was neat and cleanly in his person. He was of light stature, about five feet, five inches high, and had a loose, easy walk. With all his kind and friendly disposition, there was a certain degree of sadness that seemed to pervade his whole being. His association with others was marked by the great amount of information his conversation conveyed and the beauty of his musical voice. His addresses to the court and jury were characterized by a high order of oratory, with brilliant and forensic force. He was modest and reserved, never spoke ill of any one, never complained.[13]

The other Tiffin attorney who left written recollections of

Cowdery was William Harvey Gibson. It is an adequate intro-duction to note that Gibson's statue stands in front of the Seneca County courthouse. He won considerable fame as a Civil War general, but the statue commemorates his more famous achievements as an orator and nationally known cam-paign speaker in the late nineteenth century. Although Gibson was involved in a state scandal and resigned his elective office of treasurer of Ohio in 1857, he won back a creditable reputa-tion as Tiffin's most famous citizen. An active lawyer from 1845 to 1872 and a seasoned businessman afterward, he evalu-ated Cowdery from the vantage point of a fellow attorney and political opponent. In a letter designed for publication in 1892, Gibson said, "Cowdery was an able lawyer and [an] agree-able, irreproachable gentleman."[14]

Of Cowdery's considerable public service in his Tiffin career, most consistent and significant is his service as a mem-ber of the Board of School Examiners of Seneca County. Both William Lang and William H. Gibson's wife remembered his questioning them for certification to teach. Another individual of some ability attended one of these public examinations that Cowdery and two other trustees administered, and reported, "I must acknowledge myself not a little instructed, though but a spectator."[15] The court files also reveal that Cowdery was prominent in testing candidates for admission to the bar, so it is clear that he displayed lifelong interest and ability as an educator.

Several remarkable estimates of Cowdery as a person stem from his political activities in two states while out of the Church. In Tiffin, Ohio, he was regularly before the public as an active party worker, public speaker, and occasional candi-date for civil office. In 1842, 1844, and 1845, he was elected by the party township meeting as delegate to the Democratic county convention. In all these years he was named on the reso-lutions committee at the county convention because of his characteristic role as an articulate party spokesman. He was regularly sent to political rallies as a persuasive stump speaker. In 1845 he was elected as one of three township trustees, defeating his nearest opponent by a twenty-six per-cent vote margin.[16] In his last year of political activity in Tiffin, 1846, Cowdery was promoted for the office of state senator at a tri-county convention by a dozen delegates who were loyal to him through two ballots.[17] At an early point of his stay in Tiffin, Cowdery had written Brigham Young that he labored to produce "a fair reputation and a fair business,"[18] and his solid political career in Seneca County shows the continued truth of that statement.

The year that the Latter-day Saints migrated west, Cowdery moved also, mainly because of health problems (perhaps tuberculosis). He located at Elkhorn, Wisconsin, where he was attracted by the personal association and estab-lished law practice of his brother Lyman. It is characteristic that his first known letter from Wisconsin is from the state capital, where he initiated contact with a chief justice and a key Democratic editor.[19]

His career had three phases in the year spent in Wisconsin prior to his returning to the Church. First of all, he continued his profession as a lawyer. The minutes of the Walworth County commission reveal that he was granted an office in the courthouse October 3, 1847; the two known surviving issues of Elkhorn papers for that period contain his law advertise-ment: "O. Cowdery, Attorney & Counsellor at Law"; and court records include a number of his cases. Second, for a few months prior to rejoining the Church he was co-editor of the *Walworth County Democrat*.[20] A neighboring party newspaper acknowledged his appointment by observing, "Mr. Cowdery is highly spoken of as an editor."[21]

The third activity, politics, provides the most impressive evidence of what associates thought of Oliver Cowdery while he was away from the Church. With less than a year of residence in Elkhorn, he was nominated as state assemblyman in the first voting under the state constitution of Wisconsin. This election in the spring of 1848 was characterized by the predictable campaign smears for which Cowdery's Mormon background left him vulnerable.

With no copies of local newspapers of that period still available, the political infighting must be reconstructed from borrowed articles. The Whig paper of Cowdery's district first noted that Democrats had nominated "one of the three witnesses to the discovery of the Golden Plates, or Mormon Bible, by Joe Smith."[22] It next ran liberal extracts from the Book of Mormon, undoubtedly including the testimony of the Three Witnesses, which were the basis of personal sarcasm against Cowdery not only in the Elkhorn *Western Star*, but elsewhere.[23] Since the campaign was short, the timing of the vicious personal attack on Cowdery resulted in much of his defense reaching print after the election. He was defeated, but by only 40 votes out of about 500 total votes cast, which under the circumstances was both a moral victory and a vindication of the man.

Considering the unpopularity of Mormonism, Cowdery's Democratic associates might have chosen to respond to attacks on him with silence or even a disavowal of their candidate. Yet Horace A. Tenney, then editor of the important *Wisconsin Argus* in Madison and later a man of respectable public service to his state, deplored the defeat of "a man of sterling integrity, sound and vigorous intellect, and every way worthy, honest and capable."[24] Tenney had conversed with Cowdery personally, as well as corresponded with him, so his opinion is a matter of more than casual impression.

The most significant defense of Oliver Cowdery, however, came from John Breslin, his close associate in Tiffin, Ohio. Breslin had assumed the editorial post initially offered to

Cowdery and had constantly promoted and defended him in the *Seneca Advertiser*. A brilliant young man in Ohio politics, Breslin was elected in 1848 to the Ohio House of Representatives, where he was chosen speaker. He subsequently was reelected as representative and later elected state treasurer. While in that office he made private investments of state funds (an action somewhat condoned by contemporary practice), but he was ruined politically in 1857 when the money invested was uncollectible.[25] But the personal mistake of Breslin is quite irrelevant to his judgment on Cowdery prior to this scandal, especially since Breslin's open approval of Cowdery points to considerable public opinion in agreement with him. Immediately upon hearing that Cowdery's Mormonism was the basis of personal attacks upon him in Wisconsin, Breslin published an article deploring the "baseness of such a course" of attack; and in another article, entitled "Oliver Cowdery, Esq.," he insisted on the capability and integrity of his friend:

"Mr. C. was a resident among us for a period of seven years, during which time he earned himself an enviable distinction at the bar of this place and of this judicial circuit, as a sound and able lawyer, and as a citizen none could have been more esteemed. His honesty, integrity, and industry were worthy the imitation of all, whilst his unquestioned legal abilities reflected credit as well upon himself as upon the profession of which he was a member."[26]

Although Cowdery had initially planned to come back to the Church at the April conference of 1848, his Wisconsin nomination obviously altered this decision and postponed the return to late October, when he arrived at Kanesville, Iowa, the "eastern" headquarters of the Church. Migration to Utah that fall was out of the question, so economic reality dictated his wintering with Elizabeth Whitmer Cowdery's relatives some 250 miles southeast, in Richmond, Missouri. Since his chronic lung condition left him too weak to cross the plains and had reduced his finances, he was forced to continue his stay in Richmond for the year 1849. Research has so far failed to find evidence that he practiced law there. As a matter of fact, for a considerable portion of that year he was bedridden, and on March 3, 1850, his weakened physical condition brought his death.

The three Mormon periodicals noting Oliver Cowdery's death did so either in brief comment or by way of reference to his early prominence in the Church. Until his brief reunion with former friends on his return to the Church, the Latter-day Saints were basically unaware of his non-Mormon achievements. But he had created a marked impression upon leading men wherever he lived. Though briefly a resident of Richmond, where he died, the circuit court and bar awarded him the normal honor of a practicing attorney in good standing. Adjourning all business in honor of his funeral, it passed a resolution of condolence on behalf of "his afflicted widow and daughter," and expressed regret that "in the death of our friend and brother, Oliver Cowdery, his profession has lost an accomplished member, and the community a reliable and worthy citizen."[27] Perhaps it is strange to those accustomed to modern communication that publicity of his death was not given in Salt Lake City until some four months afterward, when it was printed in the first issue of the *Deseret News*. However, the news did not reach his main non-Mormon home at Tiffin, Ohio, until some eight months after his death. Breslin immediately headlined a story "Death of Oliver Cowdery," in which he expressed sorrow at the passing of "our much esteemed friend and former fellow citizen." More important than the few circumstantial details in this article is the final judgment of Oliver Cowdery by the friends who knew him best while he was out of the Church.

"His numerous acquaintances at this place will receive the

tidings of his decease with much regret. He was a man of more than ordinary ability, and during his residence among us had endeared himself to all who knew him in the private and social walks of life."[28]

Such a man publicly insisted that he and the Prophet Joseph Smith on several occasions stood in the presence of divine messengers who brought revelation and authority to establish The Church of Jesus Christ of Latter-day Saints.

NOTES

1. Although the title "assistant president" is loosely equated with "Counselor" in early sources, it is clear that Oliver Cowdery's position as "Second Elder" meant that be "preceded the counselors in the First Presidency in authority." (Joseph Fielding Smith, *Doctrines of Salvation*, comp. Bruce R. McConkie [Salt Lake City: Bookcraft, 1954] 1:212.) The main scriptural sources for this conclusion are his early designation as second in authority (D&C 20:3) and the 1841 appointment of Hyrum Smith to the "gifts of the priesthood, that once were put upon him that was my servant Oliver Cowdery" (D&C 124:95). This position was distinguished in the latter revelation from that of the counselors in the First Presidency.

2. *Messenger and Advocate* 2 (1836):236.

3. Far West Record, p. 122, also cit. *History of the Church*, 3:18.

4. Letter of Oliver Cowdery to his brothers Warren and Lyman, June 2, 1838, Far West, Mo. The letter was reproduced photographically by Stanley R. Gunn, *Oliver Cowdery* (Bookcraft: Salt Lake City, 1962), pp. 263–66.

5. The first known case is advertised under the name "L. & O. Cowdery" with the publication date of January 20, 1840, in the *Painesville Republican*. The notice of the case is preserved in the issue of January 28, 1840.

6. William Lang, who knew Cowdery personally, says that he came to Ohio as a young man "and entered the law office of Judge Bissell, a very distinguished lawyer in Painesville, Lake county, as a student, and was admitted to practice after having read the requisite length of time and passed an examination." (*History of Seneca County* [Springfield, Ohio, 1880], p. 364.) Whether Lang really knew the details of Cowdery's pre-Tiffin period is open to question. There is no evidence that Cowdery resided in Painesville, although he was undoubtedly assisted by Bissell.

7. Mary Bryant Alverson Mehling, *Cowdrey-Cowdery-Cowdray Genealogy* (1905), p. 173.

8. *Painesville Telegraph,* Nov. 29, 1838.

9. *Painesville Republican,* Sept. 26, 1839.

10. Ibid., Oct. 3, 1839.

11. "Letter from General W. H. Gibson," *Seneca Advertiser* (Tiffin, Ohio), Apr. 12, 1892.

12. *Seneca Advertiser,* Feb. 19, 1847.

13. Lang, *Seneca County,* p. 365. In evaluating Lang's opinion of Cowdery, it must be admitted that he shows a distinct critical ability in appraising the qualities of his fellow attorneys in the Seneca County bar.

14. "Letter from General W. H. Gibson," *Seneca Advertiser.*

15. *Seneca Advertiser,* Oct. 14, 1842.

16. Ibid., Apr. 11, 1845. For a fuller discussion of Cowdery's political offices in Tiffin, see Richard L. Anderson, "Oliver Cowdery, Esq.: His Non-Church Decade," *To the Glory of God* (Salt Lake City: Deseret Book Co., 1974), p. 197 ff.

17. Ibid., Aug. 7, 1846.

18. Letter of Oliver Cowdery to Brigham Young and Willard Richards, Dec. 25, 1843, Tiffin, Ohio, also cit. Gunn, *Oliver Cowdery,* p. 179.

19. "Letter from Wisconsin," May 18, 1847; *Seneca Advertiser,* June 18, 1847.

20. Issues of January 19, 1848, and August 4, 1848, contain his law advertisements. The masthead of the latter issue also lists him as co-editor.

21. *Racine Advocate,* July 26, 1848.

22. *Milwaukee Sentinel,* Apr. 13, 1848.

23. Ibid., Apr. 29, 1848.

24. *Wisconsin Argus,* May 16, 1848.

25. William H. Gibson, his brother-in-law and successor in the same office, was also discredited in this incident because he had bought time for Breslin to repay by not revealing the deficit at the beginning of his own term.

26. *Seneca Advertiser,* May 5, 1848. This article was copied verbatim as an endorsement in the *Walworth County Democrat* and then republished (May 30, 1848) by Horace A. Tenney in the *Wisconsin Argus* at Madison several weeks after Cowdery's defeat.

27. Circuit Court Record, Ray County, Missouri, Book C, p. 190 (entry Mar. 5, 1850).

28. *Seneca Advertiser,* Nov. 1, 1850.

Oliver Cowdery (1806–50)
The only surviving photograph.

4

Oliver Cowdery:
The Scribe as a Witness

Oliver Cowdery had fair warning that participation in the translation of the Book of Mormon would bring public ridicule. While teaching school and boarding with the Smith family during the winter of 1828–29, he began to hear rumors "from all quarters."[1] He was obviously a sincere believer to ignore the bitter community sentiment against the Smiths, to persist in inquiring concerning the ancient plates in the possession of the Smiths' son, and to face raw weather and muddy spring roads to travel over a hundred miles to Harmony, Pennsylvania, and offer his services as scribe in translating the religious history of several migrations to ancient America.

Probably no one gets such a brutally candid view of an executive or author as does a secretary, but Joseph Smith passed this severe test. Five years later, Oliver's memory of this time was still vivid:

"These were days never to be forgotten-to sit under the sound of a voice dictated by the *inspiration* of heaven, awakened the utmost gratitude of this bosom! Day after day I continued, uninterrupted, to write from his mouth, as he translated, with the *Urim* and *Thummim,* or, as the Nephites would have said, 'Interpreters,' the history, or record, called 'The Book of Mormon.' "[2]

The above statement is an important part of Oliver Cowdery's testimony as a Book of Mormon witness. Three full months of constant companionship with the translator of the record convinced this intelligent man of the inspired nature of the process by which the Book of Mormon was produced.

His official testimony, however, went far beyond this. Persecution in Pennsylvania had forced a change of residence to the Whitmer farm in upstate New York, where continued translation reiterated the direct promise that three men should see the plates.[3] An overwhelming desire to be these three witnesses came upon Oliver Cowdery, David Whitmer, and Martin Harris. In his original version of the Church history, Joseph Smith emphasized, "they became so very solicitous and teased me so much" that he sought a revelation on the subject.[4] The result was a promise, conditioned upon faith, that these men would see the plates "with your eyes."[5] One prophecy in the Book of Mormon implied even more, since it promised that the plates would be shown "by the power of God."[6]

The most complete and dramatic account of what subsequently happened is given by Joseph Smith, who depicts the anticipation that brought the four men into the woods to pray for the fulfillment of these promises, their disappointment after repeated unsuccessful prayers, the confession of lack of faith on the part of Harris, the appearance of the angel showing the plates, and the divine voice declaring the truth of the translation and issuing a command that these witnesses "bear record of what you now see and hear."[7] The appearance of the angel, the reality of the plates, and the command of God to testify of their experience are all summarized in the official testimony that the Three Witnesses permitted to be published with their names affixed:

"And we declare with words of soberness, that an Angel of God came down from heaven, and he brought and laid before our eyes, that we beheld and saw the plates, and the engravings thereon . . . and we also know that they have been translated by the gift and power of God, for his voice hath declared it unto us; wherefore we know of a surety, that the work is true."[8]

Nothing short of biblical Christianity furnishes such a concrete statement of supernatural reality. One cannot dismiss the experience easily, for each man so testifying impressed his community with his capacity and unwavering honesty, and all three consistently reaffirmed the experience in hundreds of interviews throughout their lives. Oliver Cowdery was generally recognized by Mormon and non-Mormon alike as an astute and highly intelligent individual, and his mature life was spent in the practical vocation and avocation of law and politics. The fact that he considered the above experience the most impressive and solemn event of his life must weigh heavily in favor of the objective reality of the vision. Above all, he had the emotional and intellectual capacity to know whether he was deceived. If this vision was real to him, there is a burden upon every informed person to face the great probability that the Latter-day Saints have indeed received modern revelation.

One other possibility exists—fraud. But this is merely conceivable, for Oliver's solid career as a responsible attorney and public servant is completely inconsistent with such an assumption. Of greatest weight is the unvarying reiteration of this testimony throughout a lifetime. He told the same simple story of the vision, whether under privation, persecution, resentment against the translator of the Book of Mormon, ridicule by non-Mormons, or knowledge of imminent death.

Beyond all doubt, he was repeating his inmost convictions as he testified of the truth of the Book of Mormon.

After the translation, Oliver Cowdery faithfully recopied the manuscript and spent the following winter in the tedious work of supervising its printing. The book was offered for sale ten days before the formal organization of the Church, one week after which he preached its first public discourse. In the small group that he baptized on that day was his future wife, Elizabeth Whitmer, who personally heard the first private and public statements that he made concerning his Book of Mormon witness. Active proselyting in distributing the new scripture containing his name and testimony was soon noted in the local press with skeptical sarcasm: "The *apostle* to the NEPHITES (Cowdery) has *started* for the EAST, on board a boat, with a load of 'gOld bibles.'"[9]

By the fall of the first year of Church organization, Oliver Cowdery led out in the expansion of missionary activity beyond upstate New York. In a journey as spectacular as any of the Apostle Paul, he and three companions proceeded mainly on foot 300 miles west to Kirtland, Ohio, where they "baptized one hundred and thirty disciples in less than four weeks."[10] Adding a convert-companion, they traveled and preached another 600 miles to Saint Louis, and walked the last 300 miles to their destination, Independence, Missouri, in the face of the cold and deep snow of a bitter winter in an unsettled country.[11] Oliver did not exaggerate when he later referred to the many "fatigues and privations which have fallen to my lot to endure, for the gospel's sake."[12] Like Paul, there can be no doubt that he sacrificed for his vision. Because Kirtland was the scene of the most spectacular success of this mission, the newspapers and private records report the impact of his forceful proclamation that he had seen the angel and the plates.

An example of the unbeliever's reaction to Oliver

Cowdery comes from the Shaker community at North Union, today a part of Cleveland. The vigorous leader of that settlement was impressed by Oliver's personal manner, if not his testimony. His journal introduced the incident by reviewing that the Latter-day Saint claims "began to make a stir in a town not far from North Union, Ohio," and then described the visit of the missionaries to the Shaker settlement:

"Late in the fall a member of that society came to our house to visit the Believers. His name was Oliver Cowdery. He stated that he had been one who assisted in the translation of the golden Bible, and had seen the angel, and also had been commissioned by him to go out and bear testimony that God would destroy this generation. By his request we gave liberty for him to bear his testimony in our meetings. . . . He appeared meek and mild."[13]

Non-Mormon sources clearly demonstrate the fundamental accuracy of later reminiscences of converts of the missionaries. Out of many, perhaps the most interesting is the recollection of Philo Dibble, who lived about five miles from Kirtland. With considerable ridicule his neighbors informed him "that four men had come to Kirtland with a golden Bible and one of them had seen an angel." Dibble's reaction was one of serious curiosity, shared by his wife, and they proposed to find the fact of the matter firsthand.

"I hitched up my carriage and again drove to Kirtland, one of my neighbors accompanying us with his team and family. On arriving there, we were introduced to Oliver Cowdery, Ziba Peterson, Peter Whitmer, Jr. and Parley P. Pratt. I remained with them all day, and became convinced that they were sincere in their professions. I asked Oliver what repentance consisted of, and he replied, 'Forsaking sin and yielding obedience to the gospel.' That evening he preached at Brother Isaac Morley's and bore his testimony to the administration of an angel at noonday."[14]

Published histories adequately record the career of Oliver Cowdery as an important general authority in Missouri and then Kirtland. Because he came to be the leading writer for the Church in this period, his confidence in the truth of the Book of Mormon and the divinity of the latter-day work is repeatedly expressed. The most frequently asked question about the witnesses is: If these men had seen the angel and the plates, how could they permit themselves to leave the Church? The fundamental answer is that those who had received such special favor had special problems with egotism. Because they had seen for themselves with regard to the Book of Mormon, the time came when the majority of the witnesses considered their judgment equal to Joseph Smith's on all other matters. If specific details are different in the excommunications of Oliver Cowdery and his two brothers-in-law, David and John Whitmer, there is a common theme of a clash of wills in which these witnesses failed to acknowledge Joseph Smith in his appointed role as their leader. Yet at the peak of their personal rebellion against the Prophet, each witness insisted on the strict truth of his signed testimony. Thomas B. Marsh also allowed personal feelings to overcome his commitment to the Church, although he was president of the Twelve. He immediately sought out the witnesses through whose testimony he had been converted eight years before and asked them as fellow dissenters to tell him the truth about the origin of the Book of Mormon.

"I enquired seriously at David if it was true that he had seen the angel, according to his testimony as one of the witnesses of the Book of Mormon. He replied, as sure as there is a God in heaven, he saw the angel, according to his testimony in that book. I asked him, if so, how he did not stand by Joseph? He answered, in the days when Joseph received the Book of Mormon, and brought it forth, he was a good man filled with the Holy Ghost, but he considered he had now fallen. I interrogated Oliver Cowdery in the same manner, who answered me similarly."[15]

The impressiveness of such a testimony cannot be appreciated without knowing the spirited independence that characterizes all of Oliver Cowdery's writing and is so pronounced in his personal letters at the time of his excommunication. In one of these he insists that freedom is more important than life and declares, "I shall speak out when I see a move to deceive the ignorant."[16] There is every reason to believe that he told Marsh the full truth.

The cessation of his activity in the Church meant a suspension of his role as a witness of the Book of Mormon. Not that his conviction ceased, but he discontinued public testimony as he worked out a successful legal and political career in non-Mormon society and avoided its prejudiced antagonism by creating as little conflict as possible. Since faith in Jesus Christ was the foundation of his religion, he logically affiliated himself with a Christian congregation for a time, the Methodist Protestant Church at Tiffin, Ohio. There is no more inconsistency in this than Paul's worshiping in the Jewish synagogue, or Joseph Smith's becoming a Mason in order to stem prejudice. A late recollection of Oliver's Methodist affiliation alleged that he was willing to renounce Mormonism, but what this meant to him is much too vague to imply a denial of his testimony—at his excommunication from the Church he had resigned from membership while strongly suggesting that he did not disbelieve basic doctrines.[17] Thomas Gregg asked Cowdery's colleague in the law, William Lang, whether the former Mormon leader had "openly denounced Mormonism." The answer was that he kept this subject entirely to himself: "He would never allow any man to drag him into a conversation on the subject."[18]

One of the few exceptions to this calculated silence is Oliver Cowdery's courtroom testimony of the Book of

Mormon. Evidently it did not violate his conscience to be an inactive witness, but he would not accept the role of a denying witness in a direct confrontation where silence would strongly imply a denial. The courtroom incident is widely questioned by informed people, because it is related by a secondary source that inaccurately describes him as a prosecuting attorney (an office that he sought but failed to get) and erroneously locates his law practice in Michigan (a contradiction to his continuous residence out of the Church in Ohio and Wisconsin).

This version of the courtroom scene comes from Charles M. Nielsen, who frequently described his missionary experiences in the Midwest and the conversion in 1884 of Robert Barrington, who some forty years before had heard Oliver Cowdery's testimony at a trial. The fact that Barrington lived in Michigan at this supposed contact is inconsistent with Cowdery's probable law practice in Ohio at that time.

Furthermore, the first version that Barrington gave Nielsen (recorded in 1884 in his missionary journal) was that he had been impressed with Mormonism not by Cowdery but through one Richard Cox, a Latter-day Saint who had lived in his area but moved to California. At some stage in the telling Barrington evidently created the erroneous impression that he had heard Cowdery, so the Nielsen account is thirdhand instead of secondhand.[19] Yet history is filled with examples of authentic incidents not very accurately described, so the Nielsen account is perhaps a distant recollection of this historical incident.

The earliest known statement concerning Oliver Cowdery's courtroom testimony is from Brigham Young, who in 1855 publicly reported that Oliver was "pleading law" when he was confronted with his written testimony and asked directly about its truth. According to Brigham Young, Oliver's answer emphasized that his testimony was not a matter of belief but knowledge: "what I have there said that I saw, I know that I saw."[20] Although this account also wrongly places him as practicing law in Michigan, there is more to this story than first meets the eye. First, it is told within five years of his death, when the knowledge of his life was relatively vivid. Next, the fact that this story comes from the Young family is most significant. The person who did most to bring about his reconciliation to the Church was Phineas Young, who married Oliver's half-sister. In the decade that his brother in-law was out of the Church, Phineas kept up a constant correspondence and regular visits, reporting Cowdery's actions favorably to his brother Brigham in an attempt to bring about Oliver's reinstatement.

Other members of the Young family had details of the courtroom incident. Seymour B. Young was only eleven years of age when Cowdery returned to the Church but remembered meeting him personally then at the home of Phineas at Kanesville. He related that Oliver had been ridiculed in court by the opposing counsel for his Book of Mormon testimony and that he rose "with tears streaming down his face" and simply responded that he still believed in Mormonism, though "through my own weakness I have been disfellowshipped by that people."[21] Unquestionably such traditions in the Young family were based on direct contact with Cowdery when he was still alive, perhaps at his return.

Such an incident would certainly not enter a court record, though it clearly circulated as a story among Mormon leaders, to whom young George Q. Cannon was close, through his uncle and Nauvoo employer, John Taylor. Cannon later related that he heard the details of this incident "when I was a boy." A score of similar references in his public speeches all refer to the period prior to his Hawaiian mission in 1850. In his early twenties then, Cannon does not thereafter refer to himself as "a boy." This means that Cannon evidently heard the courtroom incident while Oliver Cowdery was still alive. Although giving a late recollection, George Q. Cannon had a remarkable intellect and a great capacity for accurate detail in his personal writing. Furthermore, his version of the courtroom incident is consistent with Oliver's conservative references to Mormonism while out of the Church and places his law practice in the right state. For these reasons, Cannon's 1881 description of the courtroom testimony of the Book of Mormon witness is probably the most correct one:

> When I was a boy I heard it stated concerning Oliver Cowdery, that after he left the Church he practiced law, and upon one occasion, in a court in Ohio, the opposing counsel thought he would say something that would overwhelm Oliver Cowdery, and in reply to him in his argument he alluded to him as the man that had testified and had written that he had beheld an angel of God, and that angel had shown unto him the plates from which the Book of Mormon was translated. He supposed, of course, that it would cover him with confusion, because Oliver Cowdery then made no profession of being a "Mormon," or a Latter-day Saint; but instead of being affected by it in this manner, he arose in the court, and in his reply stated that, whatever his faults and weaknesses might be, the testimony which he had written, and which he had given to the world, was literally true.[22]

Joseph Smith took the initiative to invite Oliver Cowdery to return to the Church in 1843, an invitation likely based on Joseph Smith's estimate that Oliver was then in the frame of mind to accept it.[23] Oliver waited another four years for some form of public apology and vindication, but then swallowed his pride by traveling to Kanesville with Phineas Young and asking for baptism. An overdone document entitled "A Confession of Oliver Overstreet" claims that Oliver Cowdery was impersonated and consequently did not return to the Church. Yet its author conveniently died "a few days after he penned the confession given above," making him definitely unavailable for further historical investigation. Whoever forged this melodramatic memoir followed the record of Reuben Miller slavishly, and did not know that Phineas Young was the main actor in the drama of reinstatement—not Miller, an incidental witness. The confession alleges that Miller supervised the impersonation and does not even mention Phineas Young.

What is factual about Oliver Cowdery's return is that the deed books at Elkhorn, Wisconsin, record that he sold his property (with Phineas Young as a witness on the deed) eighteen days before Church records report his arrival at Kanesville, that James J. Strang reluctantly admitted that he returned to the main body of the Church, that William Marks (then no friend of the Twelve) recalled that Cowdery had visited Marks in Illinois "when on his way to Council Bluffs,"[24] and that contemporary records and later recollections of numerous Latter-day Saints recall his impressive appearance and testimony there. For instance, Reuben Miller recorded the testimony of the Book of Mormon scribe in his journal at the time:

"I wrote with my own pen the entire Book of Mormon (save a few pages) as it fell from the lips of the Prophet, as he translated it by the gift and power of God, by means of the Urim and Thummim, or as it is called by that book, Holy Interpreters. I beheld with my eyes, and handled with my hands, the gold plates from which it was translated. I also beheld the Interpreters. That book is true."[25]

Oliver Cowdery's stay in Kanesville was short but impressive. He consulted officially with the members of the local presidency, Orson Hyde and George A. Smith, whom he had known at Kirtland and who wrote letters at the time referring to his reconciliation. He met in formal session with the high council and high priests quorum, and the records of both bodies describe close questioning of the Book of Mormon witness by former associates who knew him at the height of his

Church career and at his apostasy. Oliver Cowdery spoke publicly in meetings after his return. John Needham, a prominent merchant in Kanesville, later recalled, "I heard him preach many time[s], and listened to his powerful testimony with regard to the work of God, Joseph Smith the Prophet, and the great events he took part in."[26]

The most intimate portrait of the Kanesville stay is from the son and daughter-in-law of Oliver's former associate in the First Presidency, Frederick G. Williams. Henrietta Williams was recovering from her first childbirth eight days previously and remembered the absence of her mother-in-law and husband to attend the conference at which Oliver spoke and the fact that "after that meeting the Cowderys stayed at our house." This included the family group: "Oliver, his wife and daughter Maria, only child living."[27] What impressed Ezra Williams most about the former priesthood leader was "the humble spirit, the realization of what he had lost by leaving the Church."[28]

The above sources on Oliver's return and reaffirmed testimony are a selection from many documents that demonstrate these events beyond reasonable question. This was actually the crescendo of an eventful career, for his chronic illness restricted his activity and then terminated his life only sixteen months after the reconciliation at Kanesville. David Whitmer concisely summed up this closing period: "In the winter of 1848, after Oliver Cowdery had been baptized at Council Bluffs, he came back to Richmond to live, and lived here until his death, March 3, 1850.[29]

In Richmond, Missouri, time was strangely turned back to Oliver's close association with the Whitmer family during the translation of the Book of Mormon in their home in upstate New York twenty years earlier. The friends of that period and their families now cared for him. At his deathbed stood David Whitmer, John Whitmer, Hiram Page and his son, the son of

Jacob Whitmer (and probably the father), as well as Phineas Young, Lucy Cowdery Young, and the wife of Oliver Cowdery. All report the power of his dying testimony, with subtle details that supplement each other. Oliver Cowdery distinctly reiterated his firm witness of the Book of Mormon with full knowledge that he faced the closing hours and moments of life.

Of the group then surrounding him, the person with most intimate knowledge of all his actions and attitudes was his wife, Elizabeth Whitmer Cowdery. Thirty-seven years later the unwavering consistency of Oliver Cowdery's testimony of the angel and the plates stood out in her mind. In a letter to her brother David Whitmer, she emphasized the meaning of the life of her husband in the measured prose that reflects his own words:

"From the hour when the glorious vision of the Holy Messenger revealed to mortal eyes the hidden prophecies which God had promised his faithful followers should come forth in due time, until the moment when he passed away from earth, he always without one doubt or shadow of turning affirmed the divinity and truth of the Book of Mormon."[30]

NOTES

1. *Biographical Sketches,* p. 128.

2. *Latter-day Saints' Messenger and Advocate* 1 (1834):14.

3. *Times and Seasons* 3 (1842):897, also cit. *History of the Church* 1:52–53.

4. *Ibid.*

5. D&C 17:1–3 (Kirtland ed. 42:1–2). Cp. ch. 1, n. 16.

6. 2 Ne. 27:12, Ether 5:3 (1830 ed., pp. 110, 548).

7. *Times and Seasons* 3:897–98, also cit. HC 1:54–56.

8. The Testimony of Three Witnesses, at end of the original edition and in the forepart of the present Book of Mormon. My quotation inverts the sequence of two thoughts but quotes precisely the words of description, which are the same in the original and present editions of the Book of Mormon.

9. *The Reflector* (Palmyra, N.Y.), June 1, 1830. The quotation has limited historical value in tracing Oliver Cowdery's early missionary work. Perhaps it merely refers to a journey to the neighboring Fayette area, conveniently accessible on the Erie Canal. He never left rural New York in this period.

10. *The Evening and the Morning Star* 1 (Apr., 1833):84. Since the editor, W.W. Phelps, did not associate himself with the Church until about a year after the Lamanite mission, these inner details of the earliest Church history probably come from his associate Oliver Cowdery.

11. See *Times and Seasons* 3 (1841):623–24, for Parley P. Pratt's summary of the final hardships of their journey: "[I]n 1830, in the depth of a howling winter five men penetrated Missouri's wilds, and traveled on foot from St. Louis to Independence, Jackson county, wading in snow to the knees and the greater part of the way for 300 miles, and all this as may be said, without money or friends, except as they made them."

12. *Latter Day Saints' Messenger and Advocate* 1 (1834):14.

13. Journal of Ashbel Kitchell, copied by Henry C. Blinn, manuscript on file at the Shaker Museum, Old Chatham, New York. A variant copy of the same journal is also at Old Chatham, made by Elisha D. Blakeman; this was published by Robert F. W. Meader, "The Shakers and the Mormons," *The Shaker Quarterly* 2 (1962):87. I have used the Blinn account because it has minor details not in Blakeman, and Mr. Meader (to whom I am indebted for manuscript copies and private correspondence) suggests that Blinn is more likely to be a careful copyist. For the spelling of Cowdery's name, Blinn has "Cowdrel" and Blakeman writes "Lowdree"; both are understandable misreadings in cursive copying from the name Cowdery. The location of Union Village is within the present Shaker Heights, a suburb of Cleveland, Ohio.

14. "Philo Dibble's Narrative," *Early Scenes in Church History*, Faith-Promoting Series, no. 8 (Salt Lake City, 1882), pp. 75–76. David Whitmer rather consistently gave noon as the approximate time of the appearance of the angel with the plates.

15. "History of Thomas Baldwin Marsh," written Nov., 1857. This was printed first in the *Deseret News*, Mar. 24, 1858, and then in *Millennial Star* 26 (1864):406.

16. Letter of Oliver Cowdery to Brothers Warren and Lyman, Feb. 4, 1838, Far West, Mo., "Cowdery Letter Book" at Huntington Library, San Marino, Calif.

17. The conclusion of Cowdery's forceful letter of resignation from the Church contained this significant sentence: "I beg you, sir, to take no view of the foregoing remarks, other than my belief on the outward government of this Church." Far West Record, p. 122, also cit. HC 3:18.

18. Letter of William Lang to Thomas Gregg, Nov. 5, 1881, Tiffin, Ohio, cit. Charles A. Shook, *The True Origin of the Book of Mormon* (Cincinnati, 1914), p. 56. There is every reason to trust Lang's personal reminiscences but every reason to distrust Lang's theories on the origin of the Book of Mormon, which he admits Cowdery discussed with no person while living in Tiffin.

19. Nielsen reported to President Heber J. Grant in a letter of Nov. 11, 1899, that he had visited Barrington in Salt Lake City, who told the courtroom story and described himself and Cox as spectators. This variation from what Barrington evidently reported to Nielsen at his conversion may suggest that Barrington was not consistent in the details of his recollection.

20. Journal of Discourses 2:258.

21. LDS Conference Report, (Apr., 1921), pp. 114–16.

22. JD 22:254. Note that the Cannon version contains the elements of testimony and personal regret of being out of the Church that are found separately in the Brigham Young and Seymour B. Young accounts. Several letters from Cowdery in the period while out of the Church deplore the circumstances that brought about his estrangement from the Church. See n. 23.

23. The Prophet's direction to the Twelve to write a letter of invitation to Cowdery is found in HC 5:368. The proof that Cowdery was willing to entertain seriously the idea of return is his emotional answer written on Christmas, 1843, from Tiffin, Ohio, to Brigham Young and the Twelve. Deeply appreciative of an earlier letter from them containing "feelings of friendship and kindness," he portrays himself as a success but a stranger in non-Mormon society, suggests an apology due for misstatements about him, and concludes by expressing to these men his "kindness, friendship and fellowship."

24. Letter of William Marks to James M. Adams, June 11, 1855, Shabbona Grove, DeKalb Co., Ill. The original has evidently perished, but a typescript of the entire letter is preserved at the RLDS Archives. Also cit. Inez Smith Davis, *The Story of the Church* (Independence, Mo., 1964), p. 420.

25. Journal of Reuben Miller, Oct. 21, 1848. For an insight into Miller's competence as a diarist, see Richard L. Anderson, "Reuben Miller, Recorder of Oliver Cowdery's Reaffirmations," *Brigham Young University Studies* 8 (1968):277–93.

26. Life Sketch of John Needham, given on his eightieth birthday anniversary to his family (Apr. 1, 1899), also cit. Andrew Jenson, *Latter-day Saint Biographical Encyclopedia* (Salt Lake City, 1901) 1:416.

27. The impersonation theory breaks down completely in the face of family relationships, Will someone now seriously suggest that Cowdery's wife and daughter were also impersonated? Numerous former friends, including the Youngs and the widow and son of Frederick G. Williams, could certainly identify each of the Cowderys. This is a good case in point on the essential difference between authentic and invented documents. The latter inevitably lack the subtle details that reflect an accurate knowledge of their surroundings. The entire Overstreet confession is bent toward explaining a single impersonation on one public occasion. Historical sources show that Cowdery's stay at Kanesville was more prolonged than this, that he was prominent in numerous meetings, and that his family accompanied him.

28. Frederick G. Williams Family Record, pp. 233–34, 246, summarized in Nancy Clement Williams, *After One Hundred Years* (Independence, Mo., 1951), pp. 148–49.

29. David Whitmer, *An Address to Believers in the Book of Mormon* (Richmond, Mo., 1887), p. 1.

30. Letter of Elizabeth Cowdery to David Whitmer, Mar. 8, 1887, Southwest City, Mo., published by George W. L. Sweich in *The Return* 3 (1892):9. In the period of his editorship, Sweich, who was the grandson of David Whitmer, published a number of family reminiscences and evidently obtained this letter from his grandfather's papers. Because it is obviously badly copied, I have corrected one spelling error, changed "shudder of turning" to "shadow of turning," and punctuated the sentence correctly.

D. WHITMER. .W. HWEICH

THE OLD RELIABLE,

Livery ᴬɴᴅ Feed Stable

DAVE WHITMER & CO.,

Proprietors,

RICHMOND, MO.

ARE prepared at any and all times to accommodate the public with

Hacks, Buggies,
and Saddle Horses!

Will convey passengers to any point desired at a moments notice Horses boarded by the day, week or month, on reasonable terms: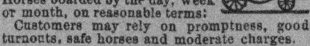
Customers may rely on promptness, good turnouts, safe horses and moderate charges.

☞ Stable near the Shaw House.

David Whimer's business advertisement, Richmond, Missouri
The form in 1882 in the Richmond Conservator.

5

David Whitmer:
Independent Missouri Businessman

Each witness of the Book of Mormon was an individualist. In David Whitmer, this quality verged on the stubborn. Whether in Mormon society or not, he stood like a rock for his principles. This outspoken and utterly honest personality would have been the first to detect fraud and expose it. During eight years in the Church and fifty years of strict separation from it, he maintained without compromise that he had seen the angel and the plates. Only a survey of his life will adequately portray an individual who did not use words lightly. The strength of the testimony is the power of the man.

By birth a Pennsylvania German, David Whitmer still betrayed "a German twang" in his conversation with George Q. Cannon in 1884. The family moved about 1809 to wooded farmland adjoining Seneca Lake in western New York. A reporter obtained from the family the description of David's father as a "hard-working, God-fearing man," who was "a strict Presbyterian and brought his children up with rigid sectarian discipline."[1] These qualities, broadened by the humaneness of the restored gospel, characterized the witness-son. Since he was a natural leader all of his life, it is significant that the first mention of him in his community is his election March 12, 1825, as sergeant in the newly organized militia company, the "Seneca Grenadiers."[2] He was then a bachelor-farmer of twenty.

His subsequent investigation and acceptance of Joseph Smith were painted in bold colors in the interviews of his elderly life. All was still vivid to him then: rumors of the "Gold Bible"; contact with the teacher Oliver Cowdery, who was traveling to Pennsylvania to see for himself; two letters from the young schoolmaster expressing firm conviction that Joseph Smith had the plates and enclosing samples of their translation; a third letter from friend Oliver requesting the hospitality of the Whitmer home. David made a 200-mile trip with team and wagon to move the translators to his home, and had intimate contact with their work, events that in later life still glowed with the power of God's assistance.[3] By June of 1829 he had given his name to the world to declare that he saw an angel exhibit the plates and heard the voice of God declare the translation correct.

David Whitmer's association with Mormonism from 1829 to his excommunication in 1838 can be itemized with a little labor. It included sustained missionary journeys, pioneering in newly settled western Missouri, and administering the affairs of the Church in the trusted inner circle of the Prophet. In these eight years no more than that many men were as prominent as was David Whitmer. The pinnacle of his recognition was the office of president of the Church in Missouri, the equivalent of a stake president in terms of current Church organization, but then of such status that the First Presidency and the Missouri presidency both sat on the stand at the Kirtland Temple dedication.

What of the man himself? When mobs terrorized the

Missouri Whitmer settlement, burning homes and brutally whipping men, it was David who vigorously organized the resistance. Two years later in Kirtland the lesson of the absence of civil protection was still vivid, and David was named "captain of the Lord's host."[4] The appointment was merely the token of a plan, not a reality, but the recognition underlines the Prophet's respect for David's courage and reliability. Joseph Smith measured the men about him well, and his opinion of David was recorded in a blessing given in 1835, the peak year of the witness's service to the Church. A few phrases from the copy that David treasured for over forty years capture his basic nature. Beloved as "a faithful friend to mankind," his integrity causes "all his words" to be as "steadfast as the pillars of heaven." "His character" will be unspotted, and "his testimony shall shine as fair as the sun, and as a diamond, it shall remain untarnished."[5] As far as the intent of that blessing, David's continued faithfulness was a condition of its complete fulfillment, but from the point of view of the man's nature, his developed personality at age thirty is depicted, which even in rebellion against the Church was not radically modified.

Tragic events culminated in David Whitmer's excommunication April 13, 1838. In the previous year of doctrinal and financial trial, prominent dissenters moved in open council to depose the Prophet and replace him with David Whitmer, a commentary on the public stature of the latter.[6] Long afterwards the witness denied certain stories of his apostasy, and gave his own version of the processes of his thinking.[7] In summary, he resisted change and was jealous of the power and suspected influence of Sidney Rigdon: "Rigdon was a thorough Bible scholar, a man of fine education, and a powerful orator. He soon worked himself deep into Brother Joseph's affections, and had more influence over him than any other man living."[8]

At David Whitmer's excommunication, the main charge was "possessing the same spirit with the dissenters."[9] This meant that he was skeptical of the new policies of the Kirtland era and had declared doctrinal and economic independence. But David really sought to re-create the intimate days of 1829–30 at his father's home in Fayette, New York. His later writings idealize this period when he felt closest to God and the Prophet. So David Whitmer is really a man who declined to grow with the Church. His grandson defined his position as "standing still."[10] If skeptical of further revelations, he nevertheless accepted the founding guidance of the Church—his letter of withdrawal in 1838 alleged a treatment inconsistent with "the revelations of God, which I believe."[11] Although the Whitmers succumbed to McLellin's flattery in 1846–47 and joined that reorganization, David soon confessed that he had been emotionally moved instead of divinely directed—so he continued to wait. This position plus opposition to polygamy characterized his family flock, the "Church of Christ" in north-central Missouri.

David Whitmer's separation just preceded Mormon expulsion from Missouri. The estranged witness remained behind to live a half-century in a society hostile to his religious views, a situation that continually highlighted his rugged independence. Two examples stand out, although the Whitmer modesty makes it necessary for the historian to piece each event together. In indignant rebuttal to the charge that he had contributed to Mormon persecution, David gave background details of an incident of the year of his excommunication: "[W]hen I came to Richmond, General Parks . . . *pressed* me and my team into service, and *I was forced to go and drive a wagon load of baggage* to Far West. I told them *if I had to go* I would take no gun. They said 'all right'; and I took no gun."[12] A reporter recorded David's recollection of the heroic sequel: "During the melee that followed he was handed a musket by the soldiery and ordered to shoot Joseph Smith, but threw the musket down, declaring he 'would not harm the Lord's anointed.' "[13]

David Whitmer also risked his life for his allegiance as a firm Unionist in a divided county in the Civil War. His family knew of his open declaration of loyalty to Lincoln,[14] and his grandson alluded to personal danger at that time: "He looked up the cocked gun barrel of the brutal men the times produced."[15] These traditions tend to confirm a detailed story from an unidentified Ray County resident. This 1888 recollection concerns a meeting where the majority began to frame resolutions requiring non-secessionists to leave the county:

"At this point in the proceedings David Whitmer arose, walked to the platform, and delivered a short but very telling speech. He stated that no resolutions or threats would cause him to run away. He declared that he was a citizen of the United States, and should remain such. He proposed to live or die under the old flag. If anyone desired to shoot him, then was a good time. The resolutions were not passed, the meeting adjourned to a given day, but did not convene."[16]

The quiet but immovable ways of David Whitmer turned grudging respect to admiration during the fifty years of his residence in Richmond, Missouri. Three decades of surviving newspapers chronicle many ordinary activities, supplemented by public documents. By his recollections his sole capital in 1838 was a wagon and team. The census records value his real estate at $1,000 in 1850, and his personal and real property in 1860 as $5,000, increasing to $7,000 in 1870. His private assets at death in 1888 were probably worth $10,000.

Perhaps general hauling work continued for some time, since he gave no specific occupation on the 1850 census. By 1860 he is listed as a "Livery Keeper," and his newspaper notices are fairly continuous for a quarter of a century for the

"Livery and Feed Stable" of "D. Whitmer & Son" or "Whitmer & Co." The editor of the *Conservator* regularly editorialized for his advertiser: "They have everything all O.K. in their line, and can furnish customers with anything from a saddle horse to a four-horse coach at a moment's notice."[17] For over two decades David Whitmer's advertisement had the same closing message: "Customers may rely on promptness, good turnouts, safe horses, and moderate charges."[18] After a time both editor and paid notices refer to the business as "The Old Reliable Livery and Feed Stable." This title symbolized the record of the firm and is really a comment about its owner.

David Whitmer's business interests were broad, and so was his service and friendship to his community. What the Whitmers did commercially for Richmond was summarized accurately by David's great-granddaughter:

"They filled hauling contracts, rented out carriages and buggies, and met two trains a day at Lexington junction with a beautifully decorated yellow bus. . . . Side lines were feed and grain, sand and gravel."[19]

David was public-spirited, serving on fair boards, and he and his wife entered competition and won prizes. Named in the newspapers as participating in many public meetings, he appears as the elected chairman of some. Shortly after the Civil War he signed as one of the "friends of Johnson, Liberty and Union,"[20] and his temperate voice was most influential in this reconstruction period. As early as 1858 he was nominated for city councilman, a position he subsequently held several times.[21] He was elected to fill the unexpired term of mayor in 1867–68, during which he sponsored several practical programs.[22] But the active businessman of sixty-three apparently retired from further office seeking; declining to attempt a second term, he recommended the election of a "younger, more energetic man." [23] His prominence, however, never diminished. The Ray County Atlas of 1877 featured his picture as one of twenty influential individuals.[24] Likenesses appeared on the same page of his lawyer-nephew, David P. Whitmer (eldest son of the witness Jacob), and Jacob T. Child, the editor of the *Richmond Conservator*.

A firm friendship existed between David Whitmer and the editor Jacob Child. This journalist was an enlightened reformer of his period and had no party connection with the Book of Mormon witness, who was thirty years his senior. Child was a forthright spokesman for the causes he championed, and one of them was supporting the integrity of David Whitmer. The opinions of "the famed publisher of the Richmond *Conservator*"[25] should carry a good deal of weight. Dynamic in local and state politics, he was elected mayor of Richmond and state assemblyman. His fellow editors named him president of the Missouri Press Association, and he was United States ambassador to Siam under President Cleveland.[26]

Some of Child's comments on David Whitmer favorably mention the Whitmer transportation business, perhaps for favors shown. A step beyond this is a definite personal relationship. For instance, during the sickness of the witness in 1881–82, Child gave regular progress reports: "We were glad to see Uncle David Whitmer on the street Monday looking remarkably well."[27] Later that year the town was excited by the marriage of David's granddaughter Josie to the brilliant young Chicago resident, James R. Van Cleave. Writing the front-page story with Victorian eloquence, the Missouri editor noticed the presence of the "silver haired patriarch, whose form is as erect and his eyes as bright as when he gazed on the Lord's messenger."[28] On several definite occasions Child went beyond such notices to openly defend the character of the Book of Mormon witness.

Whitmer's election as mayor induced some spiteful

remarks. Child's editorial reaction reminded his readers that one with "self respect" would not indulge in vicious gossip: "Mr. Whitmer is a gentleman, and as such represented the views of our people when they cast for him their votes for mayor."[29] Some fifteen years later the vitriolic anti-Mormon lecturer, Clark Braden, came to the hometown of the last Book of Mormon witness and publicly branded him as disreputable. The *Conservator*'s response was a spirited front-page editorial unsympathetic with Mormonism but insistent on "the forty six years of private citizenship on the part of David Whitmer, in Richmond, without stain or blemish."[30] Although admitting that theological views were open to question, the prominent journalist insisted that the reputation of his friend was not: "If a life of probity, of unobtrusive benevolence and well doing for well nigh a half century, marks a man as a good citizen, then David Whitmer should enjoy the confidence and esteem of his fellowmen." The following year the editor penned a tribute on the eightieth birthday of David Whitmer, who "with no regrets for the past" still "reiterates that he saw the glory of the angel."[31]

This is the critical issue of the life of David Whitmer. During fifty years in non-Mormon society, he insisted with the fervor of his youth that he knew that the Book of Mormon was divinely revealed. Relatively few people in Richmond could wholly accept such testimony, but none doubted his intelligence or complete honesty. The agnostic John Murphy from neighboring Polo, Missouri, interviewed the witness in 1880 and published his version virtually claiming David's denial. In turn, the witness businessman printed a crisp "proclamation" that he had never modified his written testimony. He also enlisted twenty-two of Richmond's political, business, and professional leaders to sign an accompanying statement that they had known him for over forty years as "a man of the highest integrity, and of undoubted truth and veracity."[32]

This certificate rightly claimed that the signers knew David Whitmer well—personal relationships can be traced in many cases, including the six that were pallbearers at his funeral seven years later. None on the list, including Jacob Child, publicly accepted the Book of Mormon, but all admired the man who testified of its truth.

The existence of witnesses of such capacity and credibility confronts every thinking person with a challenge. Those who personally talked with David Whitmer seem to have sensed the dilemma of skepticism. No one explained it more clearly than Hiram Parker, who lived in David Whitmer's section of town for a decade spanning 1870, when he listed himself on the federal census as a "marble marker and deal[er]." Later prominent in the insurance business in Detroit, Parker wrote an article around the turn of the century recalling "Uncle Davy Whitmer" and the years that they lived "side by side." Reminiscing about the appearance and personal industry of "the last living witness," who never allowed a weed to mature in his small garden, Parker tells why he was "respected by all":

"No one could know Uncle Davy and not like and trust him. . . . Children liked him, men respected him and trusted him, and I never heard a word from anyone during my ten years' acquaintance with him and those who had known him intimately for years that spoke a harsh word or uttered a doubt as to his truthfulness and general kindness of heart."[33] Parker had obviously reflected a good deal on how one might admire the man without accepting his message. Few of his townsmen could accept his Book of Mormon testimony, but "on any other subject or statement of fact neither myself or others could doubt." Hiram Parker spent most of his life in selling in several states but had never met "a more honest, guileless man"—"How one can account for the delusion that must have possessed this old man is beyond me."[34]

Such reasoning cuts two ways. Man is both a rational and a rationalizing creature. If he can invent reality, he can also explain away what has actually happened. David Whitmer insisted on the actual appearance of a supernatural being. His community insisted that he was a man of remarkable acumen and truthfulness.

At his death in 1888 a new generation of editors reiterated Richmond's judgment on the last Book of Mormon witness. The *Conservator* described David Whitmer as "one of our oldest and best known citizens,"[35] but the *Democrat* was more personal in its report.

"[N]o man ever lived here, who had among our people, more friends and fewer enemies. Honest, conscientious and upright in all his dealings, just in his estimate of men, and open, manly and frank in his treatment of all, he made lasting friends who loved him to the end."[36]

NOTES

1. *Chicago Tribune,* Dec. 17, 1885.

2. *Seneca Farmer,* Mar. 23, 1825.

3. *Kansas City Daily Journal,* June 5, 1881.

4. "The Book of John Whitmer," also cit. *Journal of History* 1 (1908):302. Cp. *History of the Church* 2:281–82.

5. The blessing, copied by David Whitmer's admirer J. L. Traughber, Jr., appeared in *The Return* 2 (1890):212–13. Its occasion appears in John Whitmer's history, pp. 302–3; the correction of two transposed words has been made from LDS records.

6. "History of Brigham Young," *Deseret News,* Feb. 10, 1858. Also cit. *Millennial Star* 25 (1863):487.

7. Whitmer stated that Lucy Smith relied upon hearsay for her reports of him in 1837. Cp. *Saints' Herald* 34 (1887):90, with *Biographical Sketches,* pp. 211–13.

8. David Whitmer, *An Address to All Believers in Christ* (Richmond, Mo., 1887), p. 35; cp. p. 59.

9. Far West Record, p. 133; also cit. HC 3:19.

10. George W. L. Sweich, *The Return* 3 (1893):1.

11. See n. 9.

12. Letter of David Whitmer to Joseph Smith III, Dec. 9, 1886, *Saints' Herald* 34 (1887):89.

13. *Chicago Tribune,* Dec. 17, 1885.

14. Helen Van Cleave Blankmeyer, *David Whitmer, Witness for God* (Springfield, Ill., 1955), pp. 51–52; cp. p. 66.

15. George W. L. Sweich, *The Return* 3 (1892):4.

16. *Chicago Times,* Jan. 26, 1888.

17. *North-West Conservator,* Aug. 12, 1865.

18. Cp., e.g., his *Conservator* advertisements of Sept. 10, 1863, with July 31, 1884.

19. Blankmeyer, *David Whitmer,* p. 50.

20. *Conservator,* Aug., 25, 1865.

21. See the *Conservator* of Apr. 9, 1858, Apr. 5, 1861, and Apr. 7, 1864. He lost by a 48–49 vote in 1858.

22. Newspaper references to Whitmer's mayorship are surveyed in Ebbie L. V. Richardson, *David Whitmer* (M.A. thesis, Brigham Young University, 1952), pp. 86–87.

23. *Richmond Conservator,* Mar. 21, 1868.

24. *Illustrated Historical Atlas of Ray County, Missouri* (Philadelphia, 1877).

25. William H. Taft, *Missouri Newspapers* (Columbia, Mo., 1964), p. 182.

26. Ibid., pp. 182, 354. Cp. *History of Ray County, Missouri* (Saint Louis, 1881), pp. 513–15.

27. *Richmond Conservator,* July 14, 1882.

28. Ibid., Nov. 17, 1882.

29. Ibid., June 22, 1867.

30. Ibid., Aug. 22, 1884.

31. Ibid., Jan. 9, 1885.

32. This statement and testimonial was published as a pamphlet and appeared in the *Richmond Conservator,* Mar. 25, 1881. Portions of the original manuscript (now at the LDS Church Historical Department) were photographically reproduced in Richardson, pp. 178–80.

33. "Mormon Reminiscences," published letter of Hiram Parker, Detroit, Feb. 15 of an unidentified year. Miss Jo Clare Mangus of Goodland, Kansas, great-granddaughter and a member of the Church, holds the original clipping. Parker died in 1921.

34. Ibid.

35. *Richmond Conservator,* Jan. 26, 1888. The editor was George W. Trigg, a signer of the 1881 testimonial.

36. *Richmond Democrat,* Jan. 26, 1888. The long story was rerun Feb. 2, 1888.

David Whitmer (1805–88) at about age seventy-two
Photograph matching the likeness in the 1877 Ray County Atlas.

6

David Whitmer:
The Most Interviewed Witness

No testimony of direct revelation in the world's history is better documented than the testimony of the Book of Mormon witnesses. Since David Whitmer was widely known as "the last-surviving witness" prior to his death in 1888, he was interviewed far more extensively than the others. He said that thousands came to inquire, and over fifty of these conversations are reported in reasonable detail in contemporary diaries, letters, and newspapers, supplemented by later recollections. This examination and cross-examination of the reports furnishes a detailed historical record. Most contain questions that one would direct to the witness, and his specific and positive answers. So today's investigator can test David Whitmer's convictions almost as well as the visitor of the past century who talked with him personally.

By means of these conversations with the last-surviving witness, one may reconstruct a line of questioning on the central points of the revelation that came to him. The following replies are taken from the better recorded interviews of about the last decade of his life. Since these responses can be documented in multiple situations, such a composite interview gives a fair idea of the impact of a private talk with David Whitmer:[1]

Q: Is your published testimony accurate?

A: "As you read my testimony given many years ago, so it stands as my own existence, the same as when I gave it, and so shall stand throughout the cycles of eternity."[2]

Q: When did this event take place?

A: "It was in June, 1829, the very last part of the month."[3]

Q: What was the approximate time of day?

A: "It was about 11 A.M."[4]

Q: What were the circumstances of the vision?

A: "[We] went out into the woods nearby, and sat down on a log and talked awhile. We then kneeled down and prayed. Joseph prayed, We then got up and sat on the log and were talking, when all at once a light came down from above us and encircled us for quite a little distance around, and the angel stood before us."[5]

Q: Describe the angel.

A: "He was dressed in white, and spoke and called me by name and said, 'Blessed is he that keepeth His commandments.' This is all that I heard the angel say."[6]

Q: Did the angel have the Book of Mormon plates?

A: "[He] showed to us the plates, the sword of Laban, the Directors, the Urim and Thummim, and other records. Human language could not describe heavenly things and that which we saw."[7]

Q: Did the vision take place under natural circumstances?

A: "The fact is, it was just as though Joseph, Oliver and I were sitting right here on a log, when we were overshadowed by a light. It was not like the light of the sun, nor like that of a fire, but more glorious and beautiful. It extended away round us, I cannot tell how far, but in the midst of this light, immediately before us, about as far off as he sits (pointing to John C. Whitmer, who was sitting 2 or 3 feet from him) there appeared, as it were, a table, with many records on it—besides the plates of the Book of Mormon, also the sword of Laban, the Directors, and the Interpreters. I saw them as plain as I see this bed (striking his hand upon the bed beside him), and I heard the voice of the Lord as distinctly as I ever heard anything in my life declaring that they were translated by the gift and power of God."[8]

Q: Can you explain the supernatural power that surrounded you?

A: "All of a sudden I beheld a dazzlingly brilliant light that surpassed in brightness even the sun at noonday, and which seemed to envelop the woods for a considerable distance around. Simultaneous with the light came a strange entrancing influence which permeated me so powerfully that I felt chained to the spot, while I also experienced a sensation of joy absolutely indescribable."[9]

Q: "Did you see the Urim and Thummim?"

A: "I saw the Interpreters in the holy vision; they looked like whitish stones put in the rim of a bow—looked like spectacles, only much larger."[10]

Q: Did you see an actual table?

A: "You see that small table by the wall? . . . Well, there was a table about that size, and the heavenly messenger brought the several plates and laid them on the table before our eyes, and we saw them."[11]

Q: Did you handle the plates?

A: "I did not handle the plates—only saw them."[12] "Joseph, and I think Oliver and Emma told me about the plates, and described them to me, and I believed them, but did not see except at the time testified of."[13]

Q: How clearly could you see the plates?

A: "[T]he angel stood before us, and he turned the leaves one by one."[14] "[H]e held the plates and turned them over with his hands, so that they could be plainly visible."[15]

Q: "Did the angel turn all the leaves before you as you looked on it?"

A: "No, not all, only that part of the book which was not sealed, and what there was sealed appeared as solid to my view as wood."[16]

Q: "Can you describe the plates?"

A: "They appeared to be of gold, about six by nine inches in size, about as thick as parchment, a great many in number and bound together like the leaves of a book by massive rings passing through the back edges. The engraving upon them was very plain and of very curious appearance."[17]

Q: Is it possible that you imagined this experience?

A: "[O]ur testimony is true. And if these things are not true, then there is no truth; and if there is no truth, there is no God; and if there is no God, there is no existence. But I know there is a God, for I have heard His voice and witnessed the manifestation of his power."[18]

Q: "Do you remember the peculiar sensation experienced upon that occasion?"

A: "Yes, I remember it very distinctly. And I never think of it, from that day to this, but what that spirit is present with me."[19]

How does one measure the truth of such testimony? The person with faith will realize (as Paul insisted) that spiritual truths must be spiritually verified. (1 Cor. 2:9–14.) Although expecting to be believed, David Whitmer advised prayer as the necessary supplement to the human testimony of witnesses: "If you are open to investigation and conviction, I pray you to read the Book of Mormon with a prayerful heart. . . . The Book carries conviction with it."[20]

Yet practical examination is the inevitable companion of a

real love for truth, and one moved by David Whitmer's testimony must subject its author to basic tests of accuracy. People in everyday life constantly sort out the valid from the invalid through the reliability of the source of information and the consistency of the report. By these standards the testimony of the last-surviving witness is trustworthy, for its author earned the solid respect of his non-Mormon townsmen through a half century of private integrity, and in this time repeated his account of the vision of the angel and the plates without varying its fundamental points. As he said himself toward the end of his life, "Those who know me best, well know that I have always adhered to that testimony."[21]

If neither the man nor his manner of relating his story is questionable, what of his motives? Can the distorting force of self-interest be detected? His plain courage in ignoring self-interest in the matter of his testimony was the source of admiration earned from community leaders in Richmond, Missouri. Neither unpopularity, danger, nor tedious inconvenience altered his expressed convictions. David occasionally alluded to an ultimatum delivered by about five hundred armed men to force him to repudiate the Book of Mormon. We know that this came in 1833 in the public square at Independence, Missouri, when vigilantes menaced Mormon leaders to force all Mormons from Jackson County. The story was told by New York convert John P. Greene, nearly as old in the Church as David Whitmer:

[W]hen the mob again assembled they went to the houses of several of the leading Mormons. And taking Isaac Morley, David Whitmer, and others, they told them to bid their families farewell, for they would never see them again. Then driving them at the point of the bayonet to the public square, they stripped and tarred and feathered them, amidst menaces and insults. The commanding officer then called twelve of his men. And ordering them to cock their guns and present them at the prisoners' breasts, and to be ready to fire when he gave the word, he addressed the prisoners, threatening them with instant death unless they denied the Book of Mormon and confessed it to be a fraud; at the same time adding that if they did so, they might enjoy the privileges of citizens. David Whitmer, hereupon, lifted up his hands and bore witness that the Book of Mormon was the Word of God. The mob then let them go.[22]

David Whitmer told Heman C. Smith that on command of the mob to "renounce his testimony," he nevertheless reaffirmed it "in the face of death."[23] The most extensive personal account of the incident was related to James H. Hart: "[T]he testimony I gave to that mob made them fear and tremble, and I escaped from them. One gentleman, a doctor, an unbeliever, told me afterwards that the bold and fearless testimony borne on that occasion and the fear that seemed to take hold of the mob had made him a believer in the Book of Mormon."[24]

In the above conversation with James H. Hart, the Missouri businessman alluded to "thousands of people" that had sought his comments, "sometimes 15 or 20 in a day." This posed no small burden on one with practical responsibilities who naturally avoided the spotlight of publicity. An example of this constant personal pressure comes from the visit of Henry Moon. One of his missionary contacts in Missouri, John Lefler, desired to talk with David Whitmer personally, and he and Moon arrived in Richmond January 9, 1872, at the inconvenient supper hour, just after dark, after an evidently difficult day of sickness in the Whitmer family. The Book of Mormon witness sought to avoid the inquirers by leaving the house to perform an errand at his livery stable, but they persistently followed him. Yet after stating that "he had not time to talk that evening," David's sense of duty about his testimony overcame his personal irritability:

We followed him in the street, and I told him that the gentleman with me had come to hear what he had to say with regard to the Book of

Mormon. I told Mr.Whitmer I had been reading the testimony of the Witnesses to Mr. Lefler, and . . . he was anxious to hear . . . for himself. 'Now Mr.Whitmer, here is the gentleman. What have you to say to him?' Mr. Whitmer turned towards Mr. Lefler and said, 'Well, God Almighty requires at my hand to bear testimony to the truth of the Book of Mormon. It is the pure Gospel of Jesus Christ, translated from the plates by the gift and power of God by Joseph Smith. . . . I know I tell the truth.'[25]

More than one person appealed privately to the last-surviving witness to disclose deceit if it existed. Two such earnest requests virtually eliminate the possibility of deception on the part of David Whitmer. James H. Moyle was later Assistant Secretary of Treasury in two U.S. administrations. Graduating with legal training at the University of Michigan in 1885, he determined to cross-examine the remaining Book of Mormon witness before returning to Utah. Young Moyle journeyed to Richmond, Missouri, secured an appointment with David Whitmer, and spent some time recounting the persecutions and sacrifices of his family because of belief in Mormonism. He further contrasted Whitmer's situation of not being far from death with his own commencement of a life's career: "And so I begged of him not to let me go through life believing in a vital falsehood." The thoughtful law student requested not confirmation, but disclosure: "Was there any possibility that he might have been deceived in any particular?" All of his life Moyle remembered the "unequivocal" affirmation of the testimony: "There was no question about its truthfulness."[26] Entries made in his diary at the time show that David Whitmer gave the young man the same information that he related to scores of others. As a mature lawyer and administrator, Moyle could not accept the view that David Whitmer misrepresented: "To have been insincere seems impossible, would have made him a hideous, soulless mental deformity."[27]

David Whitmer's grandson came to the same conclusion,

and no one seems to have been closer to the witness in his closing years than George W. Sweich, a partner in the Whitmer stables and private secretary to David. He had been personally present at numerous interviews and had written many dictated letters reaffirming his grandfather's story. Through all of this he formed his personal appraisal of the man based in large part on private conversation:

"I have begged him to unfold the fraud in the case, and he had all to gain and nothing to lose, but speak the word if he thought so. But he has described the scene to me many times, of his vision about noon in an open pasture. There is only one explanation barring an actual miracle, and that is this: If that vision was not *real*, it was HYPNOTISM, it was real to grandfather IN FACT."[28]

Since one cannot successfully challenge David Whitmer's sincerity, is there a reasonable alternative to his own explanation of the vision? Some have pointed out that the witness was as sure of certain personal revelations as his testimony of the Book of Mormon. While few fail to develop some overconfidence in their own opinions, David Whitmer never put any other incident of his life on the objective grounds of sense experience to the extent that he did his vision of the angel and the plates, Yet, in explaining that event as exceeding sense perception, David Whitmer became the target of a few who jumped to the conclusion that the revelation involved no sense perception. For instance, an interview of 1880 with John Murphy of Caldwell County was published, and David Whitmer insisted that it was erroneous. Murphy had written a tongue-in-cheek report totally emphasizing the spiritual nature of the vision. This undoubtedly distorted what David actually said, since Murphy's materialistic philosophy was not equipped to explain the miraculous. The point of misunderstanding was the choice between a vision of material plus spiritual perception or a vision of spiritual instead of material perception. The latter alternative was too quickly picked by some who talked to both Martin Harris and David Whitmer. The Missouri witness answered Murphy by a public statement "that I have never at any time denied that testimony or any part thereof."[29] The doubting Anthony Metcalf wrote to David Whitmer in 1887 and raised the same issue. The answer of the witness was a testimony of both spiritual and physical elements in the vision: "Of course we were in the spirit when we had the view, for no man can behold the face of an angel, except in a spiritual view, but we were in the body also, and everything was as natural to us, as it is at any time."[30]

John Murphy also raised the issue of whether David Whitmer had been deceived, suggesting "mesmerism" and appealing to the witness to admit that his testimony was a "delusion."[31] In terms of scientific psychology, the only person able to answer this question is David Whitmer. The possibility was put to him and ruled out many times. In this case he went to the trouble and expense of publishing his "Proclamation," repeating his testimony and emphasizing his confidence in his own powers of observation: " 'He that hath an ear to hear, let him hear;' it was no delusion!"[32]

This point is highlighted by an incident during the examination of the Book of Mormon manuscript at the Whitmer home in 1884 by a committee of the Reorganized Church of Jesus Christ of Latter Day Saints. Since this event acquired some notoriety, onlookers were often present, one of which was a skeptical Richmond military officer. The soldier discussed the Book of Mormon testimony with the aging witness in a cordial but frank manner, suggesting the possibility that Whitmer "had been mistaken and had simply been moved upon by some mental disturbance or hallucination, which had deceived him into *thinking* he saw" the angel, plates, and other objects. The immediate reaction of the witness was described by a spectator, Joseph Smith III:

"How well and distinctly I remember the manner in which Elder Whitmer arose and drew himself up to his full height— a little over six feet—and said, in solemn and impressive tones: 'No sir! I was not under any hallucination, nor was I deceived! I saw with these eyes, and I heard with these ears! *I know whereof I speak!*' "[33]

David Whitmer's "positive and emphatic testimony" solidly impressed the unbelieving questioner. For the sake of courtesy, the RLDS president left the room with the officer, who confessed the difficulty of belief "for us everyday men," but added: "[O]ne thing is certain—no man could hear him make his affirmation, as he has to us in there, and doubt for one moment the honesty and sincerity of the man himself. He fully believes he saw and heard, just as he stated he did."[34] No theme permeates the numerous Mormon and non-Mormon interviews more than this one. Few came away unimpressed with the power of David Whitmer's conviction. In 1886 Edward Stevenson visited him for the second time and talked with the feeble octogenarian, whose frame was reduced to less than a hundred pounds. Reiterating his testimony "as sure as the sun shines and I live," David Whitmer's enthusiasm had to be restrained for his own good.[35] Three years before, Moroni W. Pratt wrote about the combination of mental alertness and physical infirmity of the witness. During ordinary conversation, David would "falter a little, but when giving his testimony he would straighten up, his voice would be firm, his eye would flash, and one could feel that he spoke by the spirit of truth."[36] Independently reporting these identical details the following year, J. Frank McDowell added: "He would relate the scene with a freshness and earnestness of expression, as though it were of recent occurrence, and not of fifty-five years agone."[37]

Since genuineness is better judged by personal contact than reading cold print, these evaluations of the witness himself are as important as the record of what he said. Far from having a prepackaged statement about the Book of Mormon, David Whitmer spontaneously recalled a personal experience that deeply moved him. The believers' estimates of the witness are fully substantiated by the reactions of newspaper reporters, a class generally calloused to empty sentimentality. They measured their man during interviews and also came away impressed. A detailed and restrained report in the *Chicago Times* contained the candid opinion of the interviewer: "And no man can look at David Whitmer's face for a half-hour, while he charily and modestly speaks of what he has seen, and then boldly and earnestly confesses the faith that is in him, and say that he is a bigot or an enthusiast."[38] Joe Johnson, of the Missouri *Plattsburg Democrat,* an astute political analyst, was profoundly affected by the inner conviction of the witness. While describing the vision, David's cold symptoms diminished, "his form straightened," and with "evidently no studied effort" but with "strangely eloquent" tones, he described the vision and "the divine presence." The seasoned Missouri newspaperman classified what he heard as far more than an oddity: "Skeptics may laugh and scoff if they will, but no man can listen to Mr. Whitmer as he talks of his interview with the angel of the Lord, without being most forcibly convinced that he has heard an honest man tell what he honestly believes to be true."[39]

Those who testified to the truth of the Book of Mormon are modern witnesses not only because they lived in recent time, but also because modern investigation can study their experience. Over a hundred detailed personal statements and interviews with them exist, about half of which come from David Whitmer. Like the others, the modest but intense Missouri businessman admirably passes the test of examining his person and his story. Impeccable in reputation, consistent in scores of recorded interviews, obviously sincere, and personally capable of detecting delusion—no witness is more compelling than David Whitmer. He answered every objection thrown at him in a half century of life in Richmond, Missouri, and by sheer moral strength forced a non-Mormon community to take him seriously. Through the miracle of modern communication, his testimony now transcends a community and confronts a world.

What must be as impressive as the words of the modern witnesses is their deep sense of responsibility in reporting their experience. Despite his vigorous differences with most believers in the Book of Mormon, David Whitmer insisted that no one could evade the challenge of this modern revelation: "Kind reader, . . . beware how you hastily condemn that book which I know to be the word of God; for his own voice and an angel from heaven declared the truth of it unto me, and to two other witnesses who testified on their deathbed that it was true."[40] Less than a year after voicing this warning, David Whitmer added his deathbed testimony to the historical record. These dramatic details were published in full by the *Richmond Democrat*, but his more specific closing words were given some two weeks earlier to Angus Cannon. Bedridden and "as helpless as a child," the octogenarian was informed by George W. Sweich that his visitor wanted to hear his testimony of the Book of Mormon. After a lifetime of reiteration, the moment was still sacred to the enfeebled witness. Raising his hand, he declared: "My friend, if God ever uttered a truth, the testimony I now bear is true. I did see the angel of God, and I beheld the glory of the Lord, and he declared the record true."[41]

90

NOTES

1. If noted, a statement of David Whitmer is placed in the first person instead of the third person of a given report.

2. Letter of David Whitmer to Dr. James N. Seymour, Dec. 8, 1875, Richmond, Mo., cit. *Saints' Herald* 26 (1879):223.

3. Journal of Joseph F. Smith, cit. Joseph Fielding Smith, *Life of Joseph F. Smith* (Salt Lake City, 1938), p. 242.

4. Journal of Edward Stevenson, Dec. 22, 1877.

5. Letter of William H. Kelley to *Saints' Herald*, Jan. 16, 1882, Coldwater, Mich., cit. *Saints' Herald* 29 (1882):68.

6. Ibid.

7. Journal of George Q. Cannon, Feb. 27, 1884, cit. *Instructor* 80 (1945):520. Narrative is changed from third to first person and the clause "he said" deleted.

8. Reference at n. 3. Parenthetical definitions of "Directors" and "they" have been deleted.

9. *Omaha Herald*, Oct. 17, 1886, simultaneously released to other dailies. Narrative is changed from third to first person and the clause "Mr. Whitmer says" deleted.

10. Interview notes of Zenas H. Gurley, Jan. 14, 1885, also cit. *Autumn Leaves* 5 (1892):452.

11. Letter of James H. Hart to *Deseret News*, Aug. 23, 1883, Seneca, Mo., cit. *Deseret Evening News*, Sept. 4, 1883.

12. Journal of James H. Moyle, June 28, 1885, changed from third to first person.

13. Journal of Nathan Tanner, Jr., Apr. 13, 1886, changed from third to first person, except that the first "me" is unchanged.

14. Letter of P. Wilhelm Poulson to *Deseret News*, Aug. 13, 1878, Ogden, Utah, cit. *Deseret Evening News*, Aug. 16, 1878.

15. *Chicago Times*, Oct. 17, 1881.

16. See n. 14: Letter of P. Wilhelm Poulson to *Deseret News*, Aug. 13, 1878, Ogden, Utah, cit. *Deseret Evening News*, Aug. 16, 1878.

17. *Kansas City Daily Journal*, June 5, 1881.

18. See n. 11: Letter of James H. Hart to *Deseret News*, Aug. 23, 1883, Seneca, Mo., cit. *Deseret Evening News*, Sept. 4, 1883.

19. See n. 5: Letter of William H. Kelley to *Saints' Herald*, Jan. 16, 1882, Coldwater, Mich., cit. *Saints' Herald* 29 (1882):68.

20. David Whitmer, *An Address to All Believers in Christ* (Richmond, Mo., 1887), p. 14.

21. David Whitmer, *A Proclamation* (Richmond, Mo., 1881).

22. John P. Greene, *Facts Relative to the Expulsion of the Mormons* (Cincinnati, 1839), p. 17. This source, within six years of the event, corrects the later setting assumed in Richard Lloyd Anderson, "The Most Interviewed Witness," *Improvement Era*, May 1969, p. 79.

23. Letter of Heman C. Smith to *Saints' Herald*, June 28, 1884, Grand Prairie, Tex., cit. *Saints' Herald* 31 (1884):442.

24. See n. 11: Letter of James H. Hart to *Deseret News*, Aug. 23, 1883, Seneca, Mo., cit. *Deseret Evening News*, Sept. 4, 1883.

25. Letter of Henry Moon to Joseph F. Smith, Mar. 7, 1872, Farmington, Utah. Cp. Moon's general conference speech, *Deseret Evening News*, Apr. 10, 1872.

26. James H. Moyle, "A Visit to David Whitmer," *Instructor* 80 (1945):401.

27. Joseph E. Cardon and Samuel O. Bennion, *Testimonies of the Divinity of the Church of Jesus Christ of Latter-day Saints* (Independence, Mo., 1930), p. 305.

28. Letter of George W. Sweich, Sept. 22, 1899, Richmond, Mo., cit. 1. Woodbridge Riley, *The Founder of Mormonism* (London, 1903), pp. 219–20.

29. See n. 21: David Whitmer, *A Proclamation* (Richmond, Mo., 1881).

30. Letter of David Whitmer to Anthony Metcalf, Mar. 1887, cit. Anthony Metcalf, *Ten Years Before the Mast* (Malad, Ida., 1888), p. 74.

31. *The Hamiltonian*, Hamilton, Mo., Jan. 21, 1881.

32. See n. 21: David Whitmer, *A Proclamation* (Richmond, Mo., 1881).

33. Memoirs of Joseph Smith III, cit. Mary Audentia Smith Anderson, *Joseph Smith III and the Restoration* (Independence, Mo., 1952), pp. 311–12,

34. Ibid.

35. Letter of Edward Stevenson to Daniel H. Wells, Feb. 16, 1886, New York City, cit. *Millennial Star* 48 (1886):156.

36. Letter of Moroni W. Pratt to *Bear Lake Democrat*, July 3, 1883, Covington, Ind., cit. *Bear Lake Democrat*, July 14, 1883.

37. Letter of J. Frank McDowell to *Saints' Herald*, July 22, 1884, Olivet, Iowa, cit. *Saints' Herald* 31 (1884):508.

38. *Chicago Times*, Aug. 7, 1875.

39. *Richmond Democrat*, Jan. 26, Feb. 2, 1888, attributed to "an article written by Joe Johnson. . . ."

40. Whitmer, *Address to All Believers in Christ*, p. 43.

41. Journal of Angus Cannon, Jan. 7, 1888. Cp. Cannon's Tabernacle speech, *Deseret Evening News*, Feb. 12, 1888.

The Martin Harris farm
Air view with later farmhouse in foreground, 1978.

7

Martin Harris:
Honorable New York Farmer

The non-Mormon life of Martin Harris is slightly known but of critical importance. His character can be accurately appraised by investigating the third of a century that he lived continuously in Palmyra, New York, prior to testifying that he had seen the angel and the plates. It is unfair to this witness to fix his image as the aged survivor who came to Utah at eighty-seven and died at ninety-two. Though his memory of the rise of the Church was undimmed, he was a shadow of the prominent believer who championed the cause of Joseph Smith before a disbelieving community. Martin Harris was over twenty years older than Oliver Cowdery and David Whitmer. They reached the peak of their powers and success long after their testimony of the Book of Mormon. Harris differed from them as a substantial man of forty-six who had already achieved considerable prestige before accepting Mormonism.

His conversion to the claims of Joseph Smith caused former friends to ridicule him and produced intense domestic conflict that resulted in a separation. A highly objective survivor of this period later wrote that no early resident of Palmyra "received so many rebuffs" and endured "so many unfeeling comments" as did Martin Harris.[1] It is therefore clear that much of what was said of Martin Harris the Mormon stemmed from religious prejudice. Yet none of his townsmen exceeded his established reputation as a responsible and honest individual.

The man himself can be understood by gathering the evaluations of him made as a result of likely or demonstrated personal contact. The first anti-Mormon book, based on contemporary if generally contrived statements from the native locality of Martin Harris, admitted that "he was considered an honest, industrious citizen, by his neighbors."[2] A similar admission characterizes every major assessment of this Book of Mormon witness, even those that allege flaws in his character. The views on the man that are most significant come from about a dozen prominent acquaintances, none of whom displayed sympathy with his religious convictions.

The most detailed recollection of the background and personality of Martin Harris was printed in the *Palmyra Courier* in 1872 as part of a serial history of the town written by James H. Reeves, who was born in 1802 as a member of an early and prominent family.[3] The series included five installments devoted to Martin and his father, Nathan Harris. This is the source of most of the stories of the prowess of "Uncle Nathan" as a hunter and fisher; that pioneer is also portrayed as a vital individual who dearly loved the sociability of the frontier gatherings. The elder Harris was "universally honored by his neighbors for his kindness of heart and willingness to assist those in need." Reeves considered that Martin fell heir to "the energy and activity of his mother." Until his connection with Mormonism, which is deplored, Martin Harris "was an industrious, hard-working farmer, shrewd in his business calculations, frugal in his habits, and what was termed a prosperous man in the world."[4]

Others remembered this Book of Mormon witness on the basis of more casual contact. Stephen S. Harding, later territorial governor of Utah, recalled returning to Palmyra as a young man in 1829 to find that his birthplace was greatly affected by the appearance of the Book of Mormon. The affair "excited a good deal of curiosity and comment" mainly because "such a man as Martin Harris" was involved in it. It was "truly phenomenal" to a prejudiced community that he "should abandon the cultivation of one of the best farms in the neighborhood, and change all his habits of life from industry to indolence."[5] Both the prestige of Harris's pre-Mormon days and the contempt that many felt for him upon his conversion are revealed in this recollection.

A most valuable source of information about Martin Harris in the Palmyra community is the consistent opinion of journalists who had known him. The pioneer editor was generally an independent, tough-minded individual, and the fact that he was in the business of knowing community happenings makes all the more impressive the assessments of Martin Harris left by such men. J. A. Hadley ran one of the two major newspapers in Palmyra during the period of the production of the Book of Mormon and had personal contact with Joseph Smith and Martin Harris in considering the printing job of the Book of Mormon. He claimed to publish the first anti-Mormon news article, in 1829, in which he described Harris as "an honest and industrious farmer of this town."[6] Orsamus Turner, of fame as both editor and historian of western New York, was a printer's apprentice in Palmyra during the years 1818–20. In his admittedly sarcastic survey of Mormonism in 1852, he portrays Martin Harris as a religious fanatic, yet "an honest worthy citizen."[7]

Two printers who worked on the Book of Mormon had been formerly editors of the *Wayne Sentinel* in Palmyra. John H. Gilbert, chief compositor then, lived to tell and retell his connection with the Book of Mormon to visitors until his death in 1895. He joined the general feeling against Martin Harris as unreliable on the subject of Mormonism, but otherwise the witness was "considered by his neighbors a very honest man."[8] More prominent than Gilbert in the production of the Book of Mormon was the editorial supervisor, Pomeroy Tucker, who later gained considerable stature in western New York as a politician and editor for forty years. He published his memoirs of Mormonism in 1867, in which he intermixes his personal recollections with community hearsay in a rambling fashion. Yet he did know Harris personally, as he states in his preface, having been brought into close contact in both negotiations and printing during the winter of 1829–30. Accepting the standard non-Mormon view of the fanaticism of Harris, Tucker nevertheless evaluates him personally as "honest and benevolent." He also gives his estimation of Harris's practical abilities: he was "a prosperous, independent farmer, strictly upright in his business dealings."[9]

Such solid admiration for Martin Harris's ordinary life and career must be founded upon definite achievement. These are very important to trace from the time of his majority in 1804 until 1829, the critical year when he became a Book of Mormon witness. This period is remote and its records are incomplete, but investigation furnishes clear outlines of his occupational success and community service. These historical realities of his life definitely confirm his community reputation as a responsible, trustworthy citizen.

Martin Harris was a farmer of marked ability. For two decades prior to 1829, he had managed over 240 acres of productive land, together with associated interests. The first indication that Martin ran his own farming operation is the registration of his earmark for animals on May 22, 1808, two months after his marriage to Lucy Harris.[10] Land records show that he received the first deeds to the above tract in 1813 and 1814, but it is very probable that he had farmed this land earlier and simply received his title then.

The Ontario County Agricultural Society was not organized until 1819, and after 1823 Palmyra belonged to Wayne County, which lacked such an association in the remainder of Martin Harris's Palmyra residence. During this period of probable participation, he is visible. He won two fair prizes in 1822, eight in 1823, and three in 1824. He was named as one of the two town managers of the society for Palmyra in 1823. His prominence gives some insight into his farming activity. Since he was named in 1824 to judge swine, he had obvious ability in raising animals. But his prizes in the above years are all in the category of cloth manufacturing. He produced linen, cotton and woolen ticking, blankets, and worsted and flannel fabrics. The degree of this activity points to sheep raising and regular textile manufacturing on his farm.[11] According to the contract of sale of part of his property in 1831, however, a great portion of his land was sown in wheat, then the staple crop of the area.

Included in community service must be his participation in local campaigns of the War of 1812. Although wealthy enough to engage a substitute to accept his draft assignment, he mustered and served on several occasions for defense against British forces when his region was threatened with invasion.[12] His willingness to involve himself in community causes is shown by his election with a number of very prominent Palmyrans in 1824 to raise money to aid the Greek independence movement.[13] The same point is made by his appointment in 1827 on the Palmyra "committee of vigilance" by the Wayne County anti-Masonic convention, a cause long since discredited but which then attracted many public-spirited individuals.[14]

But the most consistent community service of Martin Harris tells most about him. He was elected by his neighbors in the annual township meetings as overseer of highways for his district in the years 1811, 1813, 1814, 1815, 1825, 1827, and 1829. In almost all of the above years these officials were also assigned to be fence viewers.[15] Such positions might be compared with the function of a non-commissioned officer who deals on a familiar level with small groups and therefore must possess tact and personal respect to succeed. The overseer of highways directed the work of neighbors on the roads in his district. It is obvious that Martin Harris was not a person with talents for high leadership as much as a trustworthy local leader.

By 1829 it was well-known in Palmyra that Martin Harris believed in Joseph Smith and the golden plates. As just shown, that year his neighbors still elected him to oversee the highway work in his district. Two years before Martin Harris became a witness of the Book of Mormon, he was sworn without disqualification as a grand juror in his county. In the following year his name appears three times as a witness before the chief criminal court of his district.[16]

If the public credentials of Martin Harris are impressive, they can be verified by recovering his confidential credit report. Loan officers measure both ability and reliability in venturing money, and one of considerable stature recalled Martin Harris's loan application in detail. The Book of Mormon witness had a professional assessment from Charles Butler, who in 1830 was a lawyer and regional loan officer for the New York Life Insurance and Trust Company, and in later life was an impeccable New York financier and philanthropist. Early in 1830 it is evident that Martin Harris lacked ready cash to pay the printer of the Book of Mormon, though valuable land was pledged as security. It was probably at this time that he traveled thirty miles to Geneva to see Butler about a loan, taking with him the recommendation of the prominent Palmyra businessman Henry Jessup. Butler left several recollections of this event but comments most specifically upon the appraisal of Harris's financial and personal capacities in the following account:

"He brought a letter of introduction to me from a highly respectable citizen of that town, a Mr. Jessup, who was a leading man and an elder in the Presbyterian Church and on whose judgment I depended in respect to the character of the borrower and the value of the property in all cases of applications for loans from that quarter. From the letter of Mr. Jessup the bearer was introduced to me as a very worthy and substantial farmer, possessing a very excellent farm, which would furnish a very ample security for the amount of money which he wished to obtain, viz. $1,300.00, and he commended Mr. Harris to me as a desirable borrower."[17]

It does not particularly concern this discussion that Butler determined that the purpose of the loan was to finance the Book of Mormon and rejected the application. In another memorandum recollection, Butler reports "my agent" as indicating that "this was one of the most respectable farmers in Wayne County."[18]

The most unusual tribute to this Book of Mormon witness came in an obituary written thirty-four years before his death. Probably because of activities of another Harris, the report spread throughout U.S. newspapers in 1841 that Martin Harris had been assassinated in Illinois for lecturing against Mormonism. This was soon corrected by the *Painesville Telegraph,* which reported from Harris's residence in Ohio that he was still alive to read "what shall be said of him after his death."[19] In the meantime Alvah Strong at Rochester had relied upon the nationally circulated story of the murder and had written his detailed estimate of his former acquaintance. Strong, a distinguished editor and respected community leader in Rochester, had earlier worked as a young printer in Palmyra just after the publication of the Book of Mormon and during the peak of Martin Harris's public preaching in that community. Based upon this and other personal knowledge, he summarized the admiration for this witness and the prejudice against his testimony that characterized the community that knew him:

"We have ever regarded Mr. Harris as an honest man. We first became acquainted with him at Palmyra, in the spring of 1828, shortly after the plates from which the Book of Mormon is said to have been translated, were found. . . . Though illiterate and actually of a superstitious turn of mind, he had long sustained an irreproachable character for probity. . . . By his neighbors and townsmen with whom he earnestly and almost incessantly *labored*, he was regarded rather as being deluded himself, than as wishing to delude others knowingly; but still he was subjected to many scoffs and rebukes, all of which he endured with a meekness becoming a better cause."[20]

The only extended evaluation of Martin Harris made in the early period is also the most complimentary. His exodus from Palmyra occasioned a touching tribute placed before the public by E. B. Grandin. Editor of the *Wayne Sentinel* in the crucial years of 1827–32 and printer of the Book of Mormon, Grandin perhaps knew Harris more intimately than any other non-Mormon. Grandin's diary is still in existence for the period immediately after these events, and it reveals him as a thoughtful, religiously independent man. This editor penned a valedictory upon the occasion of Martin Harris's leaving for Ohio with other early Latter-day Saints in 1831. It is impressive that direct approval of the honesty of the financier of the Book of Mormon should come from the man who had continual business dealings with him. Martin Harris passed this practical test with distinction:

"Mr. Harris was among the early settlers of this town, and has ever borne the character of an honorable and upright man, and an obliging and benevolent neighbor. He had secured to himself by honest industry a respectable fortune—and he has left a large circle of acquaintances and friends to pity his delusion."[21]

The personal judgments on Martin Harris from his associates generally praise his character, not personal brilliance. In almost forty years' residence in Palmyra, he was admired for integrity but not trusted with offices requiring gifted leadership. Several of the editors of the period, self-taught by constant reading, considered him naive. Strong's adjective "illiterate," however, can only mean "uncultured," because Martin's pen was ready, and numerous recollections from Palmyra emphasize that he read scripture constantly and could quote the Bible from memory at astounding length. When the religious prejudice of all opinions of the honest farmer is taken into account, Martin Harris is really being called a man of the people, lacking the polish of intellectual training but admired for his solidity by many educated men. Such an individual lends great strength to the Book of Mormon, because his presence means that the Three Witnesses were in fact a cross section of their community. If ridiculed as a religious enthusiast, he is nevertheless a forthright, simple believer. It is an act of prejudice to dismiss one so clearly competent in ordinary life without seriously considering the truth of his testimony of the Book of Mormon.

Grandin's associate in the printing of the Book of Mormon perceived this issue. Pomeroy Tucker had "frequent and familiar interviews" with Martin Harris during the production of the book, and in the previous year, just weeks after the experience of Martin's seeing the angel and the plates, Tucker joined

Grandin "in the friendly admonitions vainly seeking to divert Harris from his persistent fanaticism in that losing specula- tion."[22] Martin's tenacity in these circumstances convinced Tucker that the honorable farmer "no doubt firmly believed in the genuineness of Joseph Smith's pretensions."[23] For all of his bias against the possibility of the divine origin of the Book of Mormon, Tucker lets Harris speak for himself by means of quoting his printed testimony that "by the power of God" the witnesses "saw the plates, and the engravings thereon," and heard "his voice" declare the translation correct. The reality of this experience and the honesty of Martin Harris are obviously harmonious. But if one rejects the supernatural event, he is left with the undisputed fact that the New York farmer was a man trusted implicitly by his community in business affairs. Tucker was thoughtful enough to understand the dilemma of reject- ing the printed testimony: "How to reconcile the act of Harris in signing his name to such a statement, in view of the charac- ter of honesty which had always been conceded to him, could never be easily explained."[24]

NOTES

1. *Palmyra Courier*, May 24, 1872. Cp. note 3.

2. E. D. Howe, *Mormonism Unvailed* (Painesville, Ohio, 1834), p. 13.

3. Proof that Reeves is the author of these numerous but unsigned articles comes from the *History of Wayne County, New York* (Philadelphia, 1877), p. 134, which indicates its reliance on the historical sketches in Palmyra papers in 1870–71 "from the pen of James Reeves."

4. *Palmyra Courier*, May 24, 1872.

5. Letter of S. S. Harding to Thomas Gregg, Feb., 1882, Milan, Indiana, cit. Thomas Gregg, *The Prophet of Palmyra* (New York, 1890), pp. 36–37.

6. "Golden Bible," borrowed article from the *Palmyra Freeman*, cit. *Rochester Advertiser and Telegraph*, Aug. 31, 1829.

7. O. Turner, *History of the Pioneer Settlement of Phelps and Gorham's Purchase* (Rochester, 1852), p. 215.

8. Memorandum made by John H. Gilbert, Esq., Sept. 8, 1892, Palmyra, New York. This presently exists only in a typed copy. Cit. *Deseret News* "Church Section," Aug. 15, 1942.

9. Pomeroy Tucker, *Origin, Rise, and Progress of Mormonism* (New York, 1867), pp. 41, 50.

10. The earmark registration date appears in the *Palmyra Town Record* and the wedding date in the records of application for veterans' benefits by Martin Harris, based on service in the War of 1812, U.S. General Services Administration.

11. Identical reports of the Ontario Agricultural Fair appear in the *Wayne Sentinel* (in 1822 the *Palmyra Herald*) of Nov. 6, 1822, Nov. 19, 1823, and Nov. 17, 1824, and also the *Ontario Repository* of Oct. 29, 1822, Nov. 11, 1823, and Nov. 10, 1824.

12. These details were recalled by Martin Harris and other veterans in later applications for benefits; see n. 10: The earmark registration date appears in the *Palmyra Town Record* and the wedding date in the records of application for veterans' benefits by Martin Harris, based on service in the War of 1812, U.S. General Services Administration.

13. *Wayne Sentinel,* Jan. 21, 1824.

14. *Palmyra Sentinel,* Oct. 5, 1827.

15. *Palmyra Town Record,* entries at beginning of April in each year cited.

16. Minutes of the Court of Oyer and Terminer, Book 1, Wayne County Courthouse, Lyons, New York.

17. Manuscripts of Charles Butler, Library of Congress.

18. Ibid.

19. *The Telegraph* (Painesville, Ohio), June 30, 1841.

20. *Rochester Daily Democrat,* June 23, 1841.

21. *Wayne Sentinel,* May 27, 1831.

22. Tucker, p. 4.

23. *Palmyra Courier,* June 11, 1858.

24. Tucker, p. 71.

Martin Harris (1793–1875) at about age eighty-seven
Photograph by "Savage & Ottinger," probably in 1870.

8

Martin Harris:
Certainty from the Skeptical Witness

Martin Harris was not surpassed in doubt by Thomas nor in absolute assurance by any apostle. His testimony of the Book of Mormon was ridiculed by unbelievers as superstition, but he did not reach such certainty easily, for no witness required more evidence for his faith. This successful farmer of middle age was a seasoned trader, fully aware of possible deception in a business transaction or religious experience. And his examination of Mormonism proceeded with the methodical care that built his material estate.

When he investigated Joseph Smith's claim of possessing an ancient record, Martin waited until his wife and daughter had made personal inquiries first. Only after he saw that his own family was impressed (according to an 1859 interview) did he visit the Smiths. As mentioned, in that household he "talked with them separately, to see if their stories agreed." After satisfying himself that all of the accounts of the Smiths harmonized with Joseph's, he proceeded to lift the box containing the plates, which he concluded must contain metal as heavy as lead or gold, "and I knew that Joseph had not credit enough to buy so much lead."[1]

But this was not enough. How could the untrained farmer know that Joseph's record was ancient? Apparently to satisfy his doubts on this point he took a copy of the characters transcribed from the plates to prominent linguists, including the famous Charles Anthon of Columbia College. The professor's recollection of the interview emphasized that the Book of Mormon witness had come for his opinion "as a last precautionary step"[2] in order to be sure that "there was no risk whatever in the matter"[3] before pledging his money for the printing.

Even after entering into the work of translation in 1828 as Joseph Smith's first secretary, Martin Harris was vigilant. Upon returning to the Church in 1870 Martin reminisced of these days. The summer translation project was tedious, especially to active men accustomed to physical labor, so they broke the tension by recesses at the nearby Susquehanna River, where they exercised by throwing stones into the water. Finding a stone "very much resembling the one used for translating" Martin made a substitution without Joseph Smith's knowledge. The translator became confused and then frustrated, exclaiming, "Martin! What is the matter?" His scribe's guilty expression revealed the situation to the Prophet, who demanded an explanation. Martin's answer shows how constantly the secretary was on guard against deception: "To stop the mouths of fools, who had told him that the Prophet had learned those sentences and was merely repeating them."[4]

Joseph Smith's claims were taken seriously by this mature man conditioned by life to use his analytical powers in all circumstances. But after believing for two years, the vision of June 1829 transformed faith to certainty. Harris's prior history shows why Joseph Smith singled him out on the morning of this vision as in special need to "humble yourself" and why his struggle for faith before the vision was more severe than that of his younger associates. Upon failure of repeated prayers of Joseph Smith and the witnesses, Martin acknowledged that his attitude was probably the cause of their failure to obtain the promised revelation, and he withdrew. After the angel appeared and showed the plates to the remaining group, the Prophet found Martin Harris, and after joint prayer both were overwhelmed with the same vision. Joseph Smith remembered Martin's cry of conviction: " 'Tis enough; mine eyes have beheld!"[5] The ecstasy of that experience was indelibly stamped upon the mind of the former doubter. Lucy Smith especially remembered the return of Martin Harris to the Whitmer home immediately after the vision: "He seemed almost overcome with joy, and testified boldly to what he had both seen and heard."[6] The force of this conviction never diminished in nearly a half-century's ideological transition and personal trial.

Martin Harris's certainty that he had seen the angel and the plates is verified from the beginning of his Mormon career. As offensive to unbelievers as it was convincing to believers, his testimony was sarcastically reported by the Painesville Telegraph as given publicly in a hotel on Martin Harris's arrival there: "He told all about the gold plates, Angels, Spirits, and Jo Smith. He had seen and handled them all, *by the power of God!*"[7] Others did not come to scoff. one in this category was an editor of a different temperament, W. W. Phelps. Shortly before Martin Harris left New York for his Ohio residence, Phelps (then seriously investigating Mormon claims) recorded the following impression in a private letter: "Mr. Harris, whose name is in the book, is a wealthy farmer, but of small literary acquirements; he is honest, and sincerely declares upon his soul's salvation that the book is true."[8]

Martin was inevitably subjected to cross-examination. Another like Phelps was the intelligent and perceptive Joseph Fielding, who arrived at Kirtland, Ohio, shortly after his conversion and soon afterwards reported, "Martin Harris, one of the three witnesses of the Book of Mormon, gave me a particular description of the plates and of the Urim and Thummim, etc."[9]

Although Martin Harris was honored by appointment to the first high council of the Church, his main contribution was in the missionary service of formal journeys and private conversations. He and his brother Emer baptized a hundred converts in a few weeks,[10] and Martin was imprisoned for his forthrightness in proclaiming the restored gospel.[11] But the trials of Job descended upon the Latter-day Saint community of Kirtland, and the witness was affected. The first steps toward plural marriage rankled him, and unlike Job he felt that the loss of property in the failure of the Church bank was inconsistent with divine favor. Consequently, as he explained in 1855, he "lost confidence in Joseph Smith" and "his mind became darkened."[12]

Disillusioned Mormons now tempted the witness to recant. He and other prominent dissenters in the Church were formally excommunicated in the last week of December 1837.[13] These men, who shared Martin Harris's skepticism on Church policy, admired the sweep of Mormon doctrine and were talking of forming a reorganized church that would retain the great doctrinal concepts but jettison what to them was irrational. In a private meeting in early 1838, several former leaders insisted that the Book of Mormon was "nonsense." A contemporary letter from Kirtland reported: "Martin Harris then bore testimony of its truth and said all would be damned that rejected it."[14]

Although the Latter-day Saints moved from Kirtland, Ohio, to create a dynamic history in other states, Martin Harris remained at Kirtland for the next thirty years in the condition of a fossil embedded in an earlier layer of sediment. His constant and vocal testimony to scores of visitors is all the more remarkable in the light of the psychology of the man in this period. Social pressure should have worked against his bearing testimony at all. No other Book of Mormon witness remained in Kirtland, and he had practically lost touch with them after 1840. Not only had the Latter-day Saints deserted him (in his point of view) by moving away, but his second wife, Carolyn Young, immigrated to Utah in 1856 with their children. As the years passed in Kirtland, Martin Harris was increasingly a solitary figure in non-Mormon society, which only ridiculed him for his persistence in declaring that he had seen the angel and the plates.

Martin Harris also felt strong resentment against Church leaders, in large part stemming from the blow to his ego in never being given a major office. If such thinking is obviously immature, it was nevertheless real to the man who had sacrificed domestic peace, fortune, and reputation to bring about the printing of the Book of Mormon and the founding of the Church. Real or supposed rejection breeds hostility and, at its worst, retaliation. Though such feelings were clearly held, in the face of them Martin Harris insisted that the Mormon cause was founded on objective truth as he had experienced it in his vision of 1829.

The foregoing tendencies explain the spiritual wanderlust that afflicted the solitary witness at Kirtland. In this period of his life he changed his religious position eight times, including a rebaptism by a Nauvoo missionary in 1842. Every affiliation of Martin Harris was with some Mormon group, except when he accepted some Shaker beliefs, a position not basically contrary to his Book of Mormon testimony because the foundation of that movement was acceptance of personal revelation from heavenly beings. One may well ask, since religious instability is so much in evidence, why Martin Harris did not abandon his signed testimony. Freely seeking and bound by no Mormon ties, the only constancy of this period is his witness of the Nephite record. If Martin Harris's experience was an invention or emotional aberration, why didn't it go the way of his other religious flirtations But if his doctrinal commitments in Kirtland were fickle, his testimony of the angel and the plates remained an immovable certainty.

Throughout the Ohio residence, Martin Harris was a forceful missionary for the Book of Mormon. Some two years after Joseph Smith's death the unstable Kirtland branch was largely converted to the pretensions of James J. Strang to Mormon leadership. Apparently a disciple, the Book of Mormon witness embarked for England with the Strangite leader Lester Brooks. But private correspondence from this companion proves that Martin was not committed to the Strangite cause and for this reason was hastened back to the States.[15] Yet the eyewitnesses of the mission to England in 1846 agree that he powerfully reiterated his Book of Mormon testimony.

George Mantle later recalled attending a conference in Birmingham when Martin Harris unsuccessfully demanded the right to speak and was publicly repudiated by the presiding officer, Cyrus H. Wheelock. The latter's contemporary journal confirms Mantle's recollections. These may therefore be relied upon, especially since Mantle gave a matter-of-fact report of the words of Harris "that have from that time to this remained stamped on my memory":

"When we came out of the meeting Martin Harris was beset with a crowd in the street, expecting that he would furnish them with material to war against Mormonism; but when he was asked if Joseph Smith was a true prophet of God, he answered yes; and when asked if the Book of Mormon was true, this was his answer: 'Do you know that is the sun shining on us? Because as sure as you know that, I know that

Joseph Smith was a true prophet of God, and that he translated that book by the power of God.' "[16]

After the return of Harris from England, his life continued to be centered in Kirtland, except for occasional trips to his former home in Palmyra, New York, where he still held land. Combining social visits with business, he also felt the religious duty to share his conviction with all who would listen. For instance, a Rochester editor reported such a missionary call in 1849, wherein the Book of Mormon witness supported his testimony "with the fluency and zeal of a devotee."[17] Martin Harris was a man with a burning message. While traveling to England in 1855, David B. Dille stopped at the Harris home in Kirtland and that same year recorded his visit in detail. Martin was bedfast, so sick that he had not eaten anything in three days. But he bore his testimony with enthusiasm: " 'I know that the plates have been translated by the gift and power of God, for his voice declared it unto us. . . . And as many of the plates as Joseph Smith translated I handled with my hands, plate after plate.' Then describing their dimensions, he pointed with one of the fingers of his left hand to the back of his right hand and said, 'I should think they were so long, or about eight inches, and about so thick, or about four inches.' "[18]

Many interviews with Martin note that testifying reinvigorated his weak frame, and the Dille report is impressive in this respect. The seventy-two-year-old man insisted on getting dressed at once, ordered a meal, and spent the rest of the day in animated conversation with the young missionary, even hearing him preach that evening. Dille later recalled that after this meeting, the missionary spirit of the witness was high: "Just let me go with you to England. . . . You do the preaching and I will bear testimony to the Book of Mormon, and we will convert all England."[19] This interview must be typical of a dozen recorded conversations with Martin Harris at Kirtland that are preserved in lesser detail. Scores of people talked with him directly about his testimony, which was given with consistent particulars and uncompromising conviction.

Upon his decision to return to the Latter-day Saints in Utah in 1870, the patriarch expressed his views to attentive listeners. His precise views upon returning were recorded in some detail by a disinterested reporter, thanks to the foresight of Edward Stevenson, his companion on the return trip, who arranged an interview for the *Iowa State Register* in Des Moines. These are sample impressions from the non-Mormon editor:

"Mr. Harris is now in his 88th year, though still quite vigorous and sprightly, and he is *Mormon,* soul and body. . . . The old gentleman evidently loves to relate the incidents with which he was personally connected, and he does it with wonderful enthusiasm. . . . Joseph Smith was the first to handle the tables, and Martin Harris, one of the appointed witnesses, the second. Mr. Harris describes the plates as being of thin leaves of gold, measuring seven by eight inches, and weighing altogether, from forty to sixty pounds. . . . He believes in the visitations of angels in bodily form, for he has seen and conversed with them, as he thinks, and is satisfied."[20]

Interviewed by Utah editors, listened to by thousands in two Tabernacle speeches in Salt Lake City, and in talks in wards and in private conversations, the aged Harris never tired of repeating his story. During some six weeks in Salt Lake City he stayed at the home of his grandniece, Irinda Crandall McEwan, who later recalled the numerous callers to whom Martin bore his testimony. Her speech at a family reunion was summarized by the able and objective president of Brigham Young University, Franklin S. Harris:

"[H]undreds of people came to see him, including

President Brigham Young, to talk over with him the details regarding his contact with the Book of Mormon story and of the appearance of the angel to him. She said that anyone who heard Martin Harris describe the scenes and bear his testimony to the truthfulness of the Book of Mormon could not help but be deeply impressed with his sincerity and his absolute conviction of the truth of what he was saying."[21]

As is well known, Martin Harris lived another five years in Utah and died July 10, 1875, with his lifelong testimony of the Book of Mormon upon his lips. He resided the entire time with his oldest son by Carolyn Young, Martin Harris, Jr., who lived in Smithfield until 1874 and then moved to Clarkston. Over thirty-five people have left their impressions of talking with the elderly witness during his Utah residence. When and where such interviews took place is not as important for the present purpose as what he said. A survey of his typical language reveals the positiveness of his assertions.

John Thompson, a friend in Clarkston, related that he brought two unbelievers to his notable neighbor:

"One of them asked Mr. Harris if he believed the Book of Mormon to be true, and he told them *no*. They told him they had heard that he had never denied the truth of the book. He told them that he knew it was true, and that was past believing."[22]

A half-dozen interviews report the same response. Thomas Godfrey remembered that Martin Harris insisted that "knowledge supersedes belief," because "I saw the angel and saw the plates from which the Book of Mormon was, translated and heard the voice of God declare it was translated correctly."[23] Alma L. Jensen, present on the same occasion, gave an independent recollection of the same language but remembered the additional detail that Martin Harris physically pointed to his eyes and ears while talking to emphasize the personal knowledge of his senses.[24] Robert Aveson, a lifelong printer, recalled the exact day on which he had a long interview with the ninety-one-year-old man, who "walked in a stooping position." He asked directly about seeing the plates and the angel and received the clear reply:

"It is not a mere belief, but is a matter of knowledge. I saw the plates and the inscriptions thereon. I saw the angel, and he showed them unto me."[25]

A farmer by occupation, Martin Harris worked with physical objects and nature, and these furnished the comparisons by which he emphasized the reality of his vision. Such vivid illustrations were not easily forgotten by those who listened. Edward Moroni Thurman was about twenty-five when he saw him at a blacksmith shop and asked whether the Book of Mormon was true. The reply was a question on whether Thurman could see a nearby apple tree, and he was told that the vision was as factual as that simple sight before them.[26] Accosted on the street by a group of challenging teenagers of Clarkston, the intense nonagenarian countered with the question of whether the group could see a nearby chopping block. Upon their ascent, he replied, "Well, just as plain as you see that chopping block, I saw the plates; and sooner than I would deny it I would lay my head upon that chopping block and let you chop it off."[27] Twelve-year-old William Glenn stood by as his mature companion questioned whether Martin Harris was sure that he had seen the angel and the plates, and the spirited answer made an indelible impression upon the young Scottish immigrant. Martin Harris held out his right hand and insisted:

"Gentlemen, do you see that hand? Are you sure you see it? Are your eyes playing you a trick or something? No. Well, as sure as you see my hand so sure did I see the angel and the plates."[28]

The wife of Martin's nephew asked for the truth in a private conversation and was told, "Just as sure as the sun comes up in the east and sets in the west, I did."[29] The more normal form of the latter metaphor was a certainty "as surely as the sun is shining on us," a statement that can be documented in England in 1846, in Kirtland in 1869, and in Utah in 1871. William H. Homer remembered that after Martin Harris made this comparison he added, "I might as well doubt my own existence as to doubt the divine authenticity of the Book of Mormon or the divine calling of Joseph Smith."[30]

The average Latter-day Saint who asked Martin Harris about his testimony was not a naive believer who openly or subtly asked for mere confirmation. A good share of the answers here surveyed were to questions that deliberately tested the genuineness of the experience. In the period of Martin's most complete estrangement in Kirtland, David Cannon asked "if there was any possibility of him having been deceived in regard to the visitation of an angel," and the firm response of the older man completely satisfied the cross-questioning of the independent missionary.[31] Later in Utah a highly practical man of thirty, George Godfrey, attended the venerable Harris in his last illness and deliberately waited for a semiconscious moment to suggest that his testimony was possibly based on deception. The response was vigorous:

"I know what I know. I have seen what I have seen, and I have heard what I have heard. I have seen the gold plates. . . . An angel appeared to me and others."[32]

Filled with constant missionary zeal, Martin Harris in his closing years displayed a deep desire that his message might not be limited to the few who were able to talk directly with him. John E. Godfrey remembered the spontaneous response to his visit in the last year of the witness's life: "I am pleased to have you come, and I wish I could bear my testimony to the whole world."[33] Young William Pilkington lived in the Harris home during this final period and never forgot how insistently the old man charged him to repeat to others his personal experience of seeing the angel and the plates: "And he would hold up his right hand and swear himself that he was telling the truth."[34] His bishop in Clarkston was impressed with the remarkable clarity of Martin's mind up to the end. When he reiterated his testimony in the closing days of his life, the ninety-two-year-old witness added:

"I tell you of these things that you may tell others that what I have said is true, and I dare not deny it; I heard the voice of God commanding me to testify to the same."[35]

The agreement of many interviews with Martin Harris proves that his intense certainty never varied from his vision of the angel and the plates in 1829 to the moment of his death in 1875. Exactly one-half of his ninety-two-year span preceded the vision, which came only after prayer that followed his most careful investigations of the processes of finding and translating the Book of Mormon. The doubter was transformed into an unshakable advocate, who throughout his remaining forty-six years insisted without compromise on the objective reality of his experience. Martin Harris's words in a private letter best summarize his mission as a modern witness:

"[N]o man ever heard me in any way deny the truth of the Book of Mormon, the administration of the angel that showed me the plates, nor the organization of the Church of Jesus Christ of Latter Day Saints under the administration of Joseph Smith, Jun., the prophet whom the Lord raised up for that purpose in these the latter days, that he may show forth his power and glory."[36]

NOTES

1. Joel Tiffany, "Mormonism—No. II," *Tiffany's Monthly* 4(1859):168–70.

2. Letter of Charles Anthon to E. D. Howe, Feb. 17, 1834, New York, cit. E. D. Howe, *Mormonism Unvailed* (Painesville, Ohio, 1834), p. 271.

3. Letter of Charles Anthon to Rev. Dr. Coit, Apr. 3, 1841, New York, cit. John A. Clark, *Gleanings by the Way* (New York, 1842), p. 235, 118.

4. Edward Stevenson, "One of the Three Witnesses," *Deseret News*, Dec. 13, 1881.

5. Joseph Smith, "History of Joseph Smith," *Times and Seasons* 3 (1842):898.

6. *Biographical Sketches*, p. 139.

7. *Painesville Telegraph*, Mar. 15, 1831.

8. Letter of W. W. Phelps to E. D. Howe, Jan. 15, 1831, Canandaigua, N.Y., cit. Howe, *Mormonism Unvailed*, p. 273.

9. Letter of Joseph Fielding to Parley P. Pratt, June 20, 1841, Preston, England, cit. *Millennial Star* 2 (1841):52.

10. *The Evening and the Morning Star* 1 (Feb., 1833):70.

11. Letter of Enter Harris to George James, May 7, 1833, Springville, Pa., manuscript at Harold B. Lee Library, Brigham Young University.

12. Letter of Thomas Colburn to Erastus Snow, May 2, 1855, Saint Louis, cit. *St. Louis Luminary,* May 5, 1855.

13. Letter of John Smith to George A. Smith, Jan. 1, 1838, Kirtland, Ohio, which reported: "I called the High Council together last week and laid before them the case of a company of dissenters—28 persons—whereupon after mature discussion proceeded to cut them off from the Church. The leaders were Cyrus Smalling, Joseph Coe, Martin Harris, Luke Johnson, John Boynton, and W. W. Parrish." John Smith was then a member of the First Presidency. (See HC 2:509.)

14. Letter of George A. Smith to Josiah Fleming, Mar. 30, 1838, Kirtland, Ohio.

15. Letter of Lester Brooks to James M. Adams, Jan. 12, 1847, LaPorte, Ohio, manuscript at Yale University, also cit. Milo H. Quaife, *The Kingdom of Saint James* (New Haven, Conn., 1930), p. 243.

16. Letter of George Mantle to Marietta Walker, Dec. 26, 1888, Saint Catherine, Mo., cit. *Autumn Leaves* 2 (1889):141.

17. *Rochester Daily American*, Nov. 16, 1849.

18. Statement of David B. Dille, Sept. 15, 1853, deposited in *Millennial Star Office*, cit. *Millennial Star* 21 (1859):545.

19. The History of D. B. Dille, an autobiography written about 1886, microfilm of manuscript at the Genealogical Society library, Salt Lake City.

20. *Daily Iowa State Register*, Aug. 28, 1870; also cit. Joseph Grant Stevenson, *The Stevenson Family History* (Provo, Utah, 1955) 1:156–57.

21. Signed report of Harris Family Meeting at Geneva Resort, Utah County, Utah, Aug. 3, 1928, manuscript at Harold B. Lee Library, Brigham Young University.

22. Autobiography of John Thompson, written 1922, presently owned by his daughter, Jane Dahle.

23. Affidavit of Thomas Godfrey, July 2, 1933.

24. Autobiography of Alma L. Jensen, written 1932, photocopy at Harold B. Lee Library, Brigham Young University.

25. Robert Aveson, "Three Witnesses to the Book of Mormon," *Deseret News*, Apr. 2, 1927.

26. Private family records of Edward Moroni Thurman, copied by Ray S. Thurman, Grover, Wyoming.

27. Statement of Comfort Elizabeth Godfrey Flinders to N. B. Lundwall, Sept. 2, 1943, Ogden, Utah, cit. *Assorted Gems of Priceless Value* (Salt Lake City,

28. Statement of William M. Glenn to O. E. Fischbacher, May 30, 1943, Cardston, Alberta, Canada, cit. *Deseret News,* Oct. 2, 1943.

29. Family letter of Charles Martin and Shirley Harris, Aug. 14, 1962, addressed to Joyce Harris Lillywhite.

30. William Harrison Homer, "The Passing of Martin Harris," *The Improvement Era* 29 (1926):470.

31. David H. Cannon, "A History of the Cannon Family," speech given Feb. 19, 1922, copies of which are held by descendants, also cit. *Cannon Family Historical Treasury,* ed. Beatrice Cannon Evans and Janath Russell Cannon (Salt Lake City, 1967), p. 250.

32. Affidavit of George Godfrey, Oct. 29, 1921, original still held by attesting notary John J. Shumway, Garland, Utah.

33. Affidavit of John E. Godfrey, June 2, 1933.

34. Pilkington made numerous statements, the originals of most of which are held by the LDS Church Historical Department. "The Dying Testimony of Martin Harris," quoted here, is photographically reproduced in Wayne Cutter Gunnell, "Martin Harris, Witness and Benefactor to the Book of Mormon," BYU thesis, 1955, pp. 104–11.

35. Letter of Simon Smith to President Joseph Smith III, Dec. 29, 1880, Clifton, England, *Saints' Herald* 28 (1881):43.

36. Letter of Martin Harris, Sr., to Hanna B. Emerson, Jan., 1871, Smithfield, Utah Territory, cit. *Saints' Herald* 22 (1875):630.

John Whitmer (1802–78)
Photograph taken in the 1860 period.

9

The Whitmer Family Who Handled the Plates

"We have seen and hefted . . ."
"We did handle with our hands . . ."
"We also saw the engravings . . ."
"And we lie not . . ."[1]

With these simple claims, eight farmers and artisans publicly reported that Joseph Smith had shown them ancient plates of the Book of Mormon. A practical group who worked with their hands, they were better able to evaluate the "appearance of gold" and the "curious workmanship" than eight picked at random from a modern city.

The Prophet dated the vision of the Three Witnesses in June, 1829, commenting that the "additional testimony" of the Eight took place "soon after." Lucy Mack Smith was nearby when both events took place, and she recalled that "in a few days" after the vision of the Three, the believers from Seneca County, New York, visited the Smiths in Manchester, near Palmyra. Here the "male part of the company, with my husband, Samuel, and Hyrum," went to a nearby grove where the plates were "carried," and they "looked upon them and handled them."[2]

The eight men were Christian Whitmer, Jacob Whitmer, Peter Whitmer, Jr., John Whitmer, Hiram Page, Joseph Smith, Sr., Hyrum Smith, and Samuel H. Smith. The Smiths are better known than the four Whitmer brothers and their brother-in-law, Hiram Page, and this chapter will survey the lives and testimonies of this latter group, with occasional reference to the remaining Whitmer brother, David, one of the Three Witnesses. This group resided in the same neighborhood in Fayette township, where the Church was organized at the home of the family head, Peter Whitmer, Sr. Just one week before this event, a young Baptist minister visited this household. David Marks recorded his impression of "attending a meeting in Fayette" on March 29, 1830, "at the house of Mr. Whitmer." Although this young minister seems to have been confused in some details, he remembered "two or three" of the Whitmer sons among "eight, who said they were witnesses." They had seen "certain plates of metal, having the appearance of gold. . . . These eight, we understood, were in company with Smith and three others."[3][4]

The Whitmer family had lived near Waterloo, New York, for just two decades when they extended their hospitality to Joseph Smith and believed in his divine call. In the early part of this period a standard guidebook characterized their township: "The inhabitants [are] principally of German extract, who came hither from Pennsylvania."[5] The Whitmers were of this class. In several later interviews, David gave the date of the New York move, which took place when he was four years old (1809), and the inclusion of Peter Whitmer, Jr., on the 1810 census at Fayette confirms the family tradition.[6] The proximity of the Whitmers to other pioneer settlers in the region (the Jolleys and the Schotts) through three censuses tends to show a single residence, confirmation of David's statement that the family remained in the same place until their move west with the Mormons in 1831. The deeds to Peter Whitmer came in four transactions between 1819 and 1827, but settlers of this region typically contracted for their land and farmed it for several years before gaining formal ownership.[7]

Peter Whitmer and his sons were valued citizens of their township. The father was elected overseer of highways in his district in 1826 and 1827 and was also a local school trustee. Diedrich Willers, Jr., onetime Secretary of State of New York, prepared a careful history of Fayette late in the nineteenth century and then said of Peter Whitmer, Sr.: "He is spoken of by old Fayette residents as a worthy and industrious citizen."[8] Diedrich Willers, Sr., the respected German Reformed pastor of the Whitmers, viewed Mormon converts as superstitious, which colored his comments on the elder Peter Whitmer, but he described him as "a quiet, unpretending, and apparently honest, candid, and simple-minded man."[9] Local sources indicate that the Whitmers worshiped regularly at the early log structure of Zion's Church, a German-speaking organization about a mile south of the Whitmer farm.[10]

Not only the father, but also sons Christian, Jacob, and John Whitmer are found in Willers's church records as early as 1822. In 1825, Christian and Jacob, the two oldest sons, married sisters of the prominent Schott family. That year the twenty-seven-year-old Christian Whitmer was appointed ensign, one of three commissioned officers in the company of Seneca Grenadiers of the 102d New York Regiment of militia.[11] It is clear that this oldest Whitmer son was highly responsible and a recognized leader. He was also elected as one of six constables of Fayette township in 1828 and 1829, the year he became a witness of the Book of Mormon.[12]

The newly organized Church assigned the youngest of the

Whitmer brothers, Peter Whitmer, Jr., to travel west on a mission to the Missouri frontier. The sincere preaching of the young tradesman was remembered by several. Lyman Wight recalled his testimony "that he had seen the plates."[13] Peter's terse diary recalled on occasion: "[W]e declared the Book of Mormon."[14] Following the pattern of the apostle Paul, these missionaries supported themselves during their stay in frontier Missouri. Peter Whitmer, Jr., was an accomplished tailor and at this time was hired by General Alexander Doniphan to make him a suit.[15] But something higher than an occupation was uppermost in the mind of Peter Whitmer, Jr. The brief notes of a conference speech capture his testimony and its basis after returning from this early mission:

"My beloved brethren, ever since I have been acquainted with the writing of God, I have [viewed] eternity with perfect confidence."[16]

As the program developed for settling Jackson County, the Whitmer family and others located in a special settlement in the present Kansas City area. Among them was the Book of Mormon witness Hiram Page, a native of Vermont, who had earlier moved into western New York, married Catherine Whitmer in 1825, and then resided near his wife's family in Fayette. Some of the severest Missouri persecutions came to witnesses of the Book of Mormon. Late in 1833 John Corrill reported of Christian Whitmer: "They also took him and pointed their guns at him, threatening to kill him if he did not tell them where the brethren were."[17] Another correspondent wrote in the midst of this terror: "[T]he enemy . . . had thrown down 10 or 12 houses, and nearly whipped some to death, among whom was H. Page."[18] Earlier that year, John Whitmer had joined other Mormon leaders in offering themselves as hostages to stop the abuse of their people.

In both poverty and great faith the Latter-day Saints

regrouped in Clay County after their Jackson County expulsion. All of the Whitmer witnesses were prominent enough in this early Missouri period to sit on the high council. But death removed the oldest brother, Christian, in 1835 and the youngest, Peter, in 1836, both weakened by chronic infections. Their brother-in-law Oliver Cowdery had known them intimately for years, and left the following assessment of these men and their solemn assertion:

"By many in this church, our brothers were personally known: they were the first to embrace the new covenant, on hearing it, and during a constant scene of persecution and perplexity, to their last moments, maintained its truth—they were both included in the list of the eight witnesses in the Book of Mormon, and though they have departed, it is with great satisfaction that we reflect, that they proclaimed to their last moments, the certainty of their former testimony. . . . May all who read remember the fact, that the Lord has given men a witness of himself in the last days, and that they have faithfully declared it till called away."[19]

The next casualties among the Whitmer group were spiritual. John had been a trusted missionary, and in 1838 he was Church historian and counselor to his brother David in the Missouri presidency. Because he and W. W. Phelps, the other counselor, had taken personal title to the gathering site of Far West, the resentment of the Missouri members resulted in criticism and then formal suspension of that presidency from office. Declining to be called to account economically or to personally appear at high council trials, John Whitmer was excommunicated March 10, 1838, followed by his brother David one month later. Hiram Page and Jacob Whitmer were not formally dealt with, but they took sides with their relatives and from that time were alienated from the Church. Because the Whitmer group had sacrificed so much, it is understandable in retrospect that each of these men was angered and permanently hurt at often inconsiderate treatment from former friends. This is not to justify their very real rebellion against priesthood authority, but to observe that their steadfastness in testimony is remarkable in the face of their resentment against former associates.

Hiram Page and the Whitmers remained in upper central Missouri after the Mormon expulsion. Two main changes took place in their lives. First, these men were religiously unsettled. John Whitmer recorded his deepest feelings in his manuscript history during the month of his excommunication. Referring to difficulties in "some temporal movements," he alluded to his own "expulsion," closing with his prayer for forgiveness "of my faults" and a hope of salvation "in the Kingdom of God, notwithstanding my present situation, which I hope will soon be bettered and I find favor in the eyes of God and all men his saints."[20] Such a private comment shows that the testimony of the witnesses was no facade but the expression of a profound personal experience. Subsequently, when William E. McLellin sought to enlist them in his reorganized church in 1847, they agreed to become leaders in emotion-charged circumstances. But not long after McLellin left, Hiram Page began a series of letters to Kirtland confessing that the Missouri witnesses had failed to find the true power of God in these actions. Speaking specifically for the surviving Whitmers and himself, Page admitted, "we have been lying dormant." And yet he envisioned no practical involvement, since "the way is not opened for us to organize as we would."[21] Although inactive, a decade after their apostasy the remaining Eight Witnesses still devoutly believed that God had established his latter-day work.

The second force upon the estranged witnesses was a secularization of their lives. Their essential problem was to make a living, and artificial religious convictions would certainly tend to fade to irrelevance. For instance, Jacob Whitmer settled in Richmond, Missouri, and he faced life in 1838 with few assets and a family of seven. His struggle in this period was later outlined on the basis of information from his remarkably successful lawyer-son. From 1840 to 1843 Jacob was virtually an invalid and unable to work, at the end of which period "his limited means were well nigh exhausted."[22] A shoemaker by trade, he worked from 1843 to 1845 to buy a small acreage and erect a shoe shop on it. In the next decade he evidently followed the pattern of many early tradesmen by farming during the summer and working his shop during the winter. At his death in 1856, his industry had resulted in ownership of 113 acres.[23] But alienated from his Mormon associates for eighteen years and preoccupied with material survival, Jacob Whitmer had never waned in his conviction regarding the plates. In 1888 his second son told Andrew Jenson, "My father, Jacob Whitmer, was always faithful and true to his testimony to the Book of Mormon, and confirmed it on his death bed."[24]

Hiram Page's experience paralleled that of Jacob Whitmer. Starting out again with a family of eight in 1838, he disclosed no real estate assets on the 1850 census, two years prior to his death. Although family and neighborhood tradition indicated that Page had been a doctor when young, he was evidently untrained in that field and was generally a farmer, so listing himself on the census just mentioned. Conflict with religious associates and the fight for economic survival breaks the idealism of many a man, but Hiram Page's enthusiasm for the Book of Mormon was strong in adverse circumstances. Replying directly to an inquiry about his testimony, he mentioned early spiritual experiences and reaffirmed his practical knowledge of the plates: "As to the Book of Mormon, it would be doing injustice to myself, and to the work of God of the last days, to say that I could know a thing to be true in 1830, and know the same thing to be false in 1847."[25] Hiram

Page's letters are warm toward his former associates, sending special greetings to Martin Harris, a fellow witness. His second son was twenty at his father's death in 1852 and later told Andrew Jenson: "I knew my father to be true and faithful to his testimony of the divinity of the Book of Mormon until the very last. Whenever he had an opportunity to bear his testimony to this effect, he would always do so, and seemed to rejoice exceedingly in having been privileged to see the plates."[26]

After 1856 John Whitmer was the sole survivor of the Eight Witnesses. Outliving all the rest from two to four decades, he was contacted by more people than the others and thus left more specific statements about his experience. John Whitmer's life was tragic in the sense that he was financially successful but essentially a lonely man with deep desires to share his faith in the Book of Mormon and modern revelation.

The completely candid temperament of John Whitmer furnishes one of the best tests of the truth of his claim to have seen and handled the plates. As a trusted leader on the inner circle of decisions, he was editor of the *Messenger and Advocate* almost a year. In his closing editorial in 1836, John Whitmer shared his experiences as a member of the Church "from its beginning":

"Therefore I desire to testify to all that will come to the knowledge of this address, that I have most assuredly seen the plates from whence the Book of Mormon is translated, and that I have handled these plates, and know of a surety that Joseph Smith, Jr., has translated the Book of Mormon by the gift and power of God."[27]

From this peak of conviction, the same man descended to the depths of doubt within three years. Skeptical of Joseph Smith personally because of the failure of the Kirtland Bank, and rejected by his companions in gospel service, John Whitmer made common cause with other non-Mormons in ridiculing the faith of Theodore Turley, the business agent of the Church who remained to wind up financial affairs at Far West after the Mormons were driven out. But Turley openly accused Whitmer of inconsistency. Answering in the presence of his anti-Mormon friends, the Book of Mormon witness made two revealing statements. First, he admitted, "I now say, I handled those plates; there were fine engravings on both sides. I handled them." When Turley next asked bluntly why Whitmer now doubted the work, the witness indicated his inability to translate the characters on the plates: "I cannot read it, and I do not know whether it is true or not."[28] From the strict point of view of evidence, this report is most impressive. With social pressure to deny and personal motivation to explain away his experience, John Whitmer insisted that he had in fact handled the plates.

John Whitmer stayed in Missouri and farmed land on the site of the deserted city of Far West and its temple lot. His material success is measured by his estate inventory at death, listing ownership of 625 acres, much livestock and farm equipment, to which must be added the fine two-story house that still stands. The evaluation of his community on his forty years of residence in Caldwell County is shown by the local obituary that alluded to the Mormon expulsion: "Mr. Whitmer remained at Far West and has since been a highly respected and law abiding citizen."[29]

Although rural Caldwell County was relatively inaccessible, John Whitmer told his story of seeing the plates to a variety of visitors. In 1861, Jacob Gates talked with him over four hours and wrote in his journal, "He still testified that the Book of Mormon is true and that Joseph Smith was a Prophet of the Lord. He also said that he believed that . . . Brigham Young was carrying out the doctrine and system which Joseph Smith taught but he (Whitmer) did not believe in a man's having more than one wife."[30]

Like other Book of Mormon witnesses whose lives are well-known, John Whitmer's reiteration of his testimony was a moving experience to him. Pained that he was out of the Church, this witness wept openly when William Lewis pressed the inconsistency of his inactivity: "At last he did say, wiping the tears off, that the day would come when we would all see eye to eye."[31] The bitterness of the days after his excommunication were gone, and what remained in John Whitmer's mature years was the vivid memory of participation in the translation of a record of scripture:

"[O]ld Father John Whitmer told me last winter, with tears in his eyes, that he knew as well as he knew he had an existence that Joseph translated the ancient writing which was upon the plates, which he 'saw and handled,' and which, as one of the scribes, he helped to copy, as the words fell from Joseph's lips, by supernatural or almighty power."[32]

What motivated John Whitmer to reaffirm his testimony constantly to the end of his life? Financially successful and respected by his neighbors, this quiet man shunned notoriety. Yet his support of Mormonism at the place of the worst Mormon persecutions was certain to cause prejudice against him. His actual handling of the plates is the only plausible explanation for the seriousness with which this conservative farmer shared his testimony with Mormon visitors and non-Mormon associates. One may surely rely on his ability to report whether or not he lifted and handled a metal object of substantial weight. Six months before his death, he delivered his convictions publicly at a rural Sunday morning service, reported in the local newspaper as follows:

"Mr. Whitmer is considered a truthful, honest and law abiding citizen by this community, and consequently, his appointment drew out a large audience. Mr. Whitmer stated that he had often handled the identical *golden plates* which Mr. Smith received from the hand of the angel. He said it was of pure gold; part of the book was sealed up solid, the other part was open, and it was this part which was translated. . . . Before closing he asked the audience if they would take the Book of Mormon and the Bible and compare them, and to take Paul's rule, 'To prove all things and hold fast to that which is good.' "[33]

In fellowship or alienation, youth or age, persecution, poverty or affluence, four Whitmer brothers and Hiram Page never altered their plain testimony that they handled the original metal record of the Book of Mormon.

NOTES

1. These phrases from "The Testimony of Eight Witnesses" are identical in the 1830 and present edition of the Book of Mormon. Capitals are added to the first three clauses.

2. *Biographical Sketches*, p. 140.

3. David Marks, *The Life of David Marks* (Limerick, Maine, 1831), p. 340. His language is undoubtedly inexact in implying the appearance of the angel to all witnesses.

4. David Marks, The Life of David Marks (Limerick, Maine, 1831), p. 340. His language is undoubtedly inexact in implying the appearance of the angel to all witnesses.

5. Horatio Gates Spafford, *Gazeteer of the State of New York* (Albany, 1813), p. 187.

6. *Kansas City Daily Journal*, June 5, 1881. Family tradition and the birthplace listed on the 1850 census indicate the birth of Catherine Whitmer April 22, 1807, in Pennsylvania and the birth of Peter Whitmer, Jr. September 27, 1809, in New York.

7. Seneca County Clerk's Office, Book M, p. 430; Book Q, p. 134; Book R, p. 124; Book S, p. 567.

8. Diedrich Willers, *Centennial Historical Sketch of the Town of Fayette* (Geneva, N.Y., 1900), p. 49.

9. Letter of Diedrich Willers to Ellen E. Dickinson, cit. Ellen E. Dickinson, *New Light on Mormonism* (New York, 1885), p. 249.

10. Ibid. See also Courier Printing Company (ed.), *Manual of the Churches of Seneca County* (Seneca Falls, N.Y., 1896), p. 102.

11. *Seneca Farmer* (Waterloo, N.Y.), Mar. 23, 1825.

12. Fayette Township Record, at Waterloo Library and Historical Society, Waterloo, New York. John Genung, president of the society, assisted in locating these references.

13. Journal of Lyman Wight, cit. *Saints' Herald* 29 (1882):192.

14. Peter Whitmer, Jr., "Journal," Dec. 13, 1831.

15. Interview with Alexander W. Doniphan, *Kansas City Daily Journal*, June 12, 1881.

16. Far West Record, p. 12 (Oct. 25, 1831).

17. Letter of John Corrill to Oliver Cowdery, December 1833, Liberty, Mo., cit. *The Evening and the Morning Star* 2 (Jan., 1834): 125.

18. Letter of Nov. 6, 1833, cit. ibid. (Dec., 1833), p. 119.

19. *Latter Day Saints' Messenger and Advocate* 3 (1836):426.

20. *The Book of John Whitmer*, also cit. Journal of History 1 (1908):305. The manuscript shows that these first comments, intended to close his records, were crossed off as subsequent conflict occasioned further explanation.

21. Letter of Hiram Page to Alfred Bonny et al., June 24, 1849, Richmond, Mo., cit. *The Olive Branch* 2 (1849):27–29.

22. *History of Ray County, Missouri* (Saint Louis, 1881), p. 530. This sketch is the basis of other information in this paragraph, confirmed by additional sources.

23. Probate papers, Ray County, Mo.

24. Letter of Andrew Jenson to *Deseret News*, Sept. 13, 1888, Richmond, Mo., cit. *Deseret News*, Sept. 17, 1888.

25. Letter of Hiram Page to William E. McLellin, May 30, 1847, Ray County, Mo., cit. *Ensign of Liberty* 1 (1848):63.

26. *The Historical Record* 7 (1888):614.

27. *Latter Day Saints' Messenger and Advocate* 2 (1836):236–37.

28. Memoranda of Theodore Turley, Apr. 4, 1839, also cit. HC 3:307–8.

29. *Kingston Sentinel*, cit. *Richmond Conservator*, July 26, 1878.

30. Journal of Jacob Gates, Mar. 18, 1861.

31. Letter of William Lewis to *Saints' Herald*, Nov. 29, 1877, Stewartsville, Mo., cit. *Saints' Herald* 24 (1877):381.

32. Letter of Myron Bond to *Saints' Herald*, Aug. 2, 1878, Cadillac, Mich., cit. *Saints' Herald* 25 (1878):253.

33. Article of early 1878 from the *Kingston Sentinel*, cit. *Saints' Herald* 25 (1878):57. The date and delivery of the speech on January 13, 1878, were verified in an independent letter, cit. ibid., p. 58.

Hyrum Smith (1800–44)
Oil portrait closely following Maudsley's Nauvoo profile.

10

The Smiths Who
Handled the Plates

The first believers in the Book of Mormon were members of Joseph Smith's family. But if three of the Eight Witnesses were Smiths and the remaining ones in the Whitmer circle, it does not follow that family relationship explains away their testimony. The truth of the Book of Mormon story is better attested by those who knew its events personally than by strangers to these proceedings. Including married partners, the Smiths and Whitmers comprised about two dozen adults, none of whom expressed less than complete faith in the genuineness of the translation process.

The three Smiths who formally gave their names as seeing and handling the plates were the Prophet's father, Joseph Smith, Sr.; the Prophet's older brother, Hyrum; and his immediately younger brother, Samuel Harrison. They sometimes joined the other Book of Mormon witnesses to reaffirm their testimony printed in the 1830 edition of the Book of Mormon regarding lifting and turning the leaves of the plates. After quoting the published statements of the Three and Eight Witnesses, and describing the experience of the latter group,

Lucy Smith relates, "The ensuing evening, we held a meeting, in which all the witnesses bore testimony to the facts as stated above."[1] Two years later, in the period of dynamic preaching of the early elders, a conference was held near Cleveland, Ohio, remembered by Luke Johnson as follows: "At this conference the eleven witnesses to the Book of Mormon, with uplifted hands, bore their solemn testimony to the truth of that book, as did also the Prophet Joseph."[2]

A study of the Smith witnesses must stress deeds more than words. Modest and unaffected, these men left few formal statements, but above all they lived consistently with their commitment to Christian principles and modern revelation. Although not parading their printed testimony, they sacrificed for their convictions. Their sincerity is powerful evidence for the existence of the Book of Mormon plates and more. The father and the two brothers nearest Joseph's age constantly lived and worked with him, and from this intimate vantage point completely accepted his report of his early visions.

Hyrum and Samuel Smith had joined the Presbyterian Church with their mother, who later related the visit of a church committee to persuade them to abandon their convictions about the Book of Mormon then being printed. The chief spokesman believed that "Joseph never had the plates," and asked Hyrum if he did not think himself deceived. The witness answered simply, "No sir, I do not." After unsatisfactory attempts to break down his story, similar questions were directed to Samuel, who defied his interrogators with scripture about false shepherds.[3] Local church records support such a conversation, since they refer to the visit of the committee, which reported that they "received no satisfaction" from talking with Lucy, Hyrum, and Samuel Smith.[4] The result was suspension from Presbyterian membership, a symptom of the ostracism inflicted by their community for their faith in the Book of Mormon.

In the face of ridicule and intimidation, the twenty-two-year-old Samuel Smith took copies of the new scripture to neighboring regions of western New York right after the Church was organized in April, 1830. Phineas Young later recalled the blend of humility and conviction with which the Prophet's younger brother presented the Book of Mormon. Without introduction, Samuel handed a book to Phineas with the request that he read it. Finding that it claimed to be a revelation, Phineas took the book from Samuel," and by his request looked at the testimony of the witnesses." The missionary then promised his investigator a witness from God if he would read the book prayerfully. Upon agreeing that he would, Phineas asked the name of the missionary, who only then identified himself as Samuel H. Smith. Young reported the closing words of this conversation: " 'Ah,' said I, 'You are one of the witnesses.' 'Yes,' said he, 'I know the book to be a revelation from God, translated by the gift and power of the Holy Ghost, and that my brother Joseph Smith, Jr., is a Prophet, Seer and Revelator.' "[5]

It is doubtful whether anyone exceeded Samuel Smith's record of active missionary service during the earliest years of the latter-day Church. Moving with the Saints to Ohio in 1831, he left a characteristically concise record of a two-month mission with Reynolds Cahoon in the counties around Cleveland, in which he summarized his own preaching: "I spoke of the testimony which the Lord had given to the people of this generation of his work, the fulness of the gospel, his everlasting covenant, and bore testimony of these things."[6] Scores of converts accepted the personal assurance of this plain-spoken youth who had known the events of the restoration from the beginning.

Samuel Smith's best-documented mission is one mentioned in the Doctrine and Covenants, which instructed him and Orson Hyde to "take their journey into the eastern countries, and proclaim the things which I have commanded them."[7] Both men kept journals indicating that the presentation and testimony of the Book of Mormon was one of the major themes of their preaching. The witness was ridiculed periodically for his simple reiteration of his testimony: "The people gathered around us and asked a great many questions about the plates, etc., and many of them used much lightness."[8] Daniel Tyler was converted as a result of this mission and later recalled their message in Erie County, Pennsylvania:

"In the spring of 1832, Elders Samuel H. Smith and Orson Hyde . . . came to our neighborhood and held a few meetings. Elder Smith read the 29th chapter of Isaiah at the first meeting and delineated the circumstances of the coming forth of the Book of Mormon, of which he said he was a witness. He knew his brother Joseph had the plates, for the prophet had shown them to him, and he had handled them and seen the engravings thereon. His speech was more like a narrative than a sermon."[9]

Anyone who studies the personality of Samuel H. Smith must admit that he is not likely to have invented such testimony. A dutiful son, loyal brother, and kindly father, his life is the essence of sincerity. Of sufficient capacity to be named to the first high council of the Church in 1834, and be elected by his fellow councilors as president in 1837, yet Samuel was not ambitious. When not in arduous missionary service, he farmed or hired out as a laborer. In Nauvoo he was named a bishop and was elected a city alderman. This public success marks a deep respect for him based on his character, not cleverness. His missionary companion called him "a man slow of speech and unlearned, yet a man of good faith and extreme integrity."[10] His patriarch-father blessed him as "loved of the Lord" because of his "faithfulness and truth."[11] Samuel H. Smith's inner motivation is best revealed in the minutes of an early speech, indicating that "he had set out to serve the Lord, not to regard the favor of men but the favor of heaven."[12] The consistency of his testimony and the evident honesty of the man sustain the reality of his handling the plates.

The same may be said of the Prophet's father for similar reasons. A deeply religious and humble man, Joseph Smith, Sr., was not a person who exaggerated his worth. One of his few personal statements was recorded at the crest of his service to the Church, his intense patriarchal ministry of giving blessings at Kirtland. One meets the man himself in this address to his family, just prior to blessing them in 1834. Although he had always held family scripture reading and prayer, he referred to his earlier life when the Smiths were unable to agree on the validity of any church:

"I have not always set that example before my family that I ought. I have not been diligent in teaching them the commandments of the Lord, but have rather manifested a light and trifling mind. But in all this I have never denied the Lord. Notwithstanding all this my folly, which has been a cause of grief to my family, the Lord has often visited me in visions and in dreams and has brought me, with my family, through many afflictions, and I this day thank his holy name."[13]

One so truthful about himself would not likely be a party to a religious hoax. Joseph Smith, Sr., was a practical man who never aspired to public acclaim. He had brief careers in teaching and storekeeping, but he worked with his hands most of his life as a cooper or farmer. His candid modesty endeared him to those who had intimate contact with him. His wife characterized him "an affectionate companion and tender father, as ever blessed the confidence of a family."[14] Edward

Stevenson voiced the impression of many a member of the Church: "Naturally Father Smith was not a man of many words, but, sober-minded, firm, mild and impressive."[15] Joseph Smith, Jr., considered him "a great and a good man," possessing an "exalted, and virtuous mind." This wording and the following report come from a son who knew his father's life as few individuals could: "I now say that he never did a mean act, that might be said was ungenerous in his life, to my knowledge."[16] If those nearest Joseph Smith, Sr., could invariably rely on his personal goodness and strict integrity, his printed testimony of seeing and handling the plates may not lightly be questioned.

The mainstay of those without facts is ridicule. A generation whose pious conservatism was shocked by the Mormon claim of new revelation would not allow the Smith family their just due as honest individuals. So to take certain vindictive testimonials as historical fact is the height of irresponsibility. In 1833 D. P. Hurlbut (his own spelling) forfeited his LDS membership on the ground of unrepentant adultery.[17] Turning from missionary for the new revelations to lecturer against them, he was employed by an anti-Mormon committee in Ohio to gather material to "completely divest Joseph Smith of all claims to the character of an honest man,"[18] a quest with obvious implications for the father and brothers of the Prophet. Whether Hurlbut himself had the integrity to record accurate statements may be doubted. Leading Mormons of the time insisted that his reputation was so notoriously tattered that his work had to be published by the more reputable but equally bitter E. D. Howe, who said in a later interview that "Hurlburt was always an unreliable fellow."[19]

Non-Mormon writers have admitted the need to treat the Hurlbut-Howe affidavits with extreme caution, because they were "collected by one hostile individual whose style of composition stereotypes the language of numerous witnesses."[20] This is apparent in the main thrust of every Palmyra-Manchester affidavit printed by Howe. Stock phrases allege that the Smith men were "lazy" and "indolent," having the "general employment" of "money digging." "They were a family that labored very little," so "their great object appeared to be to live without work"; consequently, it was "a mystery to their neighbors how they got their living."[21]

Such phrases are historically meaningless and merely brand the source as unreliable. From the memoirs of Lucy, Joseph, and William Smith, verified by later recollections of non-Mormon neighbors and even census reports at the time, it is known that the family was highly industrious. Their practical dependability is shown by merely listing their economic activities in western New York from 1818 to 1828, which included the following:

(1) Purchasing 100 acres of densely forested land on installments and clearing substantial portions with hand tools.

(2) Building a substantial log dwelling, followed by a frame house, farm buildings, and extensive fences.

(3) Raising wheat as a main crop, and caring for 1,500 sugar-producing trees by gathering the sap and processing sugar and molasses.

(4) Extensive manufacturing of coopering products, including barrels, baskets, and birch brooms.

(5) Supplementing income by regular hiring out as laborers and selling refreshments to crowds on holidays.

This factual reconstruction of the real activities of the Smith men in Palmyra-Manchester is supplemented by the recollections of neighbors who directly contradicted the Hurlbut-Howe testimonials. One clearly in a position to know was Orlando Saunders, who was born two years before the Prophet and worked by the side of the Smiths on the nearby farm owned by his father, Enoch Saunders, whose death in

1825 transferred the property to Orlando. Fortunately, this man was later interviewed by both believers and unbelievers in the claims of the Smith family, and he told the same story.

Reorganized *LDS Interview*	*Non-LDS Interview*
[T]hey have all worked for me many a day; they were very good people. Young Joe (as we called him then) . . . was a good worker, they all were. . . . [T]hey were poor people. . . ."[22]	"Orlando Sanders . . . tells us that the Smith family worked for his father and for himself. He gives them the credit of being good workers, but declares that they could save no money."[23]

As already mentioned, on several public occasions Joseph Smith, Sr., reiterated his witness of the plates of the Book of Mormon. His private testimony is also a matter of history. Maliciously imprisoned for debt by resentful townsmen, he was offered freedom for renouncing the Book of Mormon but instead accepted four days' starvation and thirty days' imprisonment, a fair test of his sincerity.[24] An interview with him about this time was reported from memory some forty years later. Though filled with inaccuracies (as having Joseph instead of Martin Harris take the characters to New York), this 1870 recollection reported that the Prophet's father discussed the weight, dimensions, and appearance of the plates in detail.[25] The power of his personal conviction may be measured by the fact that Joseph Smith, Sr., persuaded his parents and most of his brothers of the truth of the new revelation. The impact of his first visit was later related by George A. Smith:

"Some time in August, 1830, my uncle Joseph Smith and Don Carlos Smith came some two hundred and fifty miles from where the Prophet was residing in Ontario County, New York, and they brought a Book of Mormon with them. I had never seen them before, and I felt astonished at their sayings."[26]

The unsophisticated honesty of Joseph Smith, Sr., and Samuel H. Smith is mirrored in the sensitive reliability of the Prophet's older brother Hyrum. Somewhat better educated than the rest of his brothers, and a man of marked executive ability, he gave distinguished service from the organization of the Church until his martyrdom a decade and a half later. In the year when he became a Book of Mormon witness he was an independent farmer of twenty-nine with a wife and two children. He was respected by his neighbors, for he served as school trustee in his neighborhood in 1828.[27] Elected to this office in the local school district, he with two other trustees managed school affairs and funds, including hiring of teachers. Hyrum's non-Mormon reputation became clearer after the work of Masonic scholar Mervin Hogan, who published the Nauvoo Lodge minutes indicating that Hyrum Smith had been a Mason in good standing in the Mount Moriah lodge No. 112, which met in Palmyra, New York.[28] Further research shows that Hyrum indeed appears on the Palmyra report covering the period to June 4, 1828, just a year before he became a Book of Mormon witness. He is one of fifty-nine members, and is not named as newly initiated that year. This means that normal Masonic procedures of unanimity had admitted him on grounds that his character would honor that organization—a judgment made by the large Palmyra group, among whom were young printer Pomeroy Tucker and respected physician Alexander McIntire.[29]

The complete dedication of the Prophet's older brother to

the restored Church separated him from further success in non-Mormon society. But the power of his leadership was felt in the Mormon community as a missionary, temple builder, civic leader, patriarch, and official counselor to his Prophet-brother for about seven years, including his appointment as assistant president in closest relationship to Joseph Smith in directing the Church. No early LDS leader is spoken of in warmer terms than Hyrum Smith. After traveling with him as a missionary, Orson Hyde described Hyrum as "a pleasant and an agreeable companion, a wise counselor, a father and a guide."[30] The Prophet spontaneously picked two qualities that compelled love for his brother: "the integrity of a job, and in short, the meek and quiet spirit of Jesus Christ."[31] The numerous comments about this Book of Mormon witness generally allude to these dual qualities of honesty and kindness. The candid John Taylor found no flaw: "If ever there was an exemplary, honest, and virtuous man, an embodiment of all that is noble in the human form, Hyrum Smith was its representative."[32]

One this impressive cannot be ignored when he insists that he was not deceived in examining and lifting the Book of Mormon Plates. And his descriptions follow the same pattern of consistency of all other witnesses. A brother-in-law of Hyrum Smith, the educated Joseph Fielding, talked personally to the witness's wife and reported in 1841: "My sister bears testimony that her husband has seen and handled the plates."[33] A speech of 1844 was recalled by the capable Angus Cannon: "When I was but ten years of age, I heard the testimony of the Patriarch Hyrum Smith, one of the eight witnesses, to the divinity of the Book of Mormon and the appearance of the plates from which it was translated."[34] A public declaration of this witness in Salem, Massachusetts (perhaps 1841), was remembered in 1843 and reprinted by a non-Mormon newspaper editor:

"We have seen Hiram Smith, a brother of Jos., and heard him preach, and conversed with him about his religion, its origin and progress; and we heard him declare, in this city in public, that what is recorded about the plates, &c. &c. is God's *solemn truth.*"[35]

As stated, the essence of the Smiths' witness to the Book of Mormon plates is deeds, not words. The constancy of faithful sacrifice places a force upon their testimonies that no amount of eloquence may produce. The supernatural power of the angel's visit to the Three Witnesses finds its physical foundation in the fact that eight ordinary men insisted all of their lives that they had carefully examined and handled the ancient plates of the Book of Mormon. That practical reality is emphasized by the lives of the Smiths who handled the plates. Worn out by middle-aged privation for the cause of the restoration, Joseph Smith, Sr., died of a severe lung condition a year after the Mormon expulsion from Missouri.[36] The strain of a dangerous horseback ride in an attempt of Samuel to reach his brothers before their murder, and the shock of their deaths, brought fatal sickness to this last-surviving witness of the Smiths, who died a month later.[37] With his beloved Prophet-brother, Hyrum earlier faced the guns of a murderous mob in his last moments. And it is clear that his martyrdom meant exactly to Hyrum what the Latter-day Saints made of it. Interviews with the prison companions of Joseph and Hyrum were the basis of historical details that Hyrum read portions of the Book of Mormon the night before the martyrdom, and the next day bore testimony of the coming forth of the Book of Mormon.[38]

There is a striking parallel between the earlier Missouri imprisonment and that of Illinois. In the former case, Hyrum Smith described why he was willing to make such a sacrifice. This statement without doubt is also Hyrum's explanation of the meaning to him of his final sacrifice of life itself:

147

"Having given my testimony to the world of the truth of the Book of Mormon, . . . and the establishment of the Kingdom of Heaven, in these last days; and having been brought into great afflictions and distresses for the same—I thought that it might be strengthening to my beloved brethren, to give them a short account of my sufferings, for the truth's sake, and the state of my mind and feelings, while under circumstances of the most trying and afflicting nature. . . .

"[I] had been abused and thrust into a dungeon . . . on account of my faith. . . . However, I thank God that I felt a determination to die, rather than deny the things which my eyes had seen, which my hands had handled, and which I had borne testimony to, wherever my lot had been cast; and I can assure my beloved brethren that I was enabled to bear as strong a testimony, when nothing but death presented itself as ever I did in my life."[39]

NOTES

1. Biographical Sketches, p. 141.

2. Deseret News, May 26, 1858.

3. Biographical Sketches, p. 147.

4. Palmyra Presbyterian Session Records, vol. 2, Mar. 10, 1830. Cp. Richard

5. Autobiography of Phineas Young, also cit. Deseret News, Feb. 3, 1858.

6. Missionary record of Samuel Smith.

7. D&C 87:3 1835 ed.), 75:13 (current ed.).

8. Samuel H. Smith Journal, Sept. IS, 1832.

9. Daniel Tyler, "Incidents of Experience," Scraps of Biography, Faith-Promoting Series (Salt Lake City, 1883), 10 :23.

10. Autobiography of Orson Hyde, also cit. Deseret News, May 5, 1858.

11. Patriarchal Blessing Book 1, p. 5, also cit. Ruby K. Smith, Mary Bailey (Salt Lake City, 1954), p. 41.

12. Far West Record, p. 12 (Oct. 25, 1831).

13. Patriarchal Blessing Book 1, p. 1.

14. Biographical Sketches, p. 162.

15. "In Early Days," Juvenile Instructor, 29 (1894):552.

16. Manuscript History of the Church, Aug. 22, 1842, also cit. History of the Church 5:125–26.

17. Cp. ibid., 1:352–55, and Times and Seasons 6 (1845):784–85.

18. Painesville Telegraph, Jan. 31, 1834.

19. Ellen E. Dickinson, New Light on Mormonism (New York, 1885), p. 7

THE SMITHS WHO HANDLED THE PLATES

20. Whitney R. Cross, The Burned-Over District (Ithaca, 1950, 1965).

21. E. D. Howe, Mormonism Unvailed (Painesville, Ohio, 1834), pp. 262, 232, 251, 260, 249. Cp. Richard Lloyd Anderson, "Joseph Smith's New York Reputation Reappraised," BYU Studies 10 (1970), 283–89.

22. Interview with William H. Kelley, Saints' Herald 28 (1881):165.

23. Frederic G. Mather, "The Early Days of Mormonism," Lippincott's Magazine 26 (1880):198.

24. Biographical Sketches, p. 165.

25. Interview of Fayette Lapharn, The Historical Magazine 7 (2d ser., 1870):305 ff.

26. Journal of Discourses 5:103.

27. Biographical Sketches, p. 128.

28. Hyrum Smith assisted in the first Nauvoo Lodge activities as a member, giving his former lodge as "Mount Moriah, No. 112, N.Y." Mervin B. Hogan (ed.), Founding Minutes of Nauvoo Lodge, U.D. (Des Moines, Iowa: Research Lodge No. 2 [1971]), p. 8, Dec. 30, 1841 entry. The same entry appears in the second set of minutes; see Hogan (ed.), Official Minutes of Nauvoo Lodge, U.D. (Des Moines, Iowa: Research Lodge No. 2 [1974]), pp. 16–17.

29. See "Return of Mount Moriah Lodge No. 112, held in the town of Palmyra . . . from June 4th A.L. 5827 to June 4th A.L. 5828," examined by the suggestion of Prof. Hogan and through the courtesy of Grand Lodge Librarian Allan Boudreau, at the New York Grand Lodge, New York City. Prof. Hogan's comments on the meaning of Hyrum's membership have been most helpful.

30. Hyde, Autobiography.

31. The text follows the Kirtland Manuscript History of Warren Parrish, also cit. HC 2:338.

32. HC 7:107. Cp. p. 54.

33. Letter of Joseph Fielding to Parley P. Pratt, June 20, 1841, Preston, England, cit. L.D.S. Millennial Star 2 (1841):52.

34. Salt Lake Stake Historical Record, Jan. 25, 1888.

35. Salem Advertiser and Argus, Apr. 12, 1843, also cit. Times and Seasons 1 (1840):172 ff.

36. Funeral sermon of Robert B. Thompson, Sept. 15, 1840, Times and Seasons 1 (1840):172 ff.

37. See the contemporary description evidently originating from Lucy Smith, in the letter of H. Herringshaw to William Smith, Aug. 28, 1844, Nauvoo, Ill.

38. HC 6:600, 610.

39. General letter of Hyrum Smith, Dec., 1839, Commerce, Ill., Times and Seasons 1 (1839):20, 23.

Leonidas letter.

Oliver Cowdery, Esq.

We are gratified to learn, as we do from the Walworth (Wisconsin) Democrat, that our esteemed friend and former fellow citizen, O. COWDERY, Esq., has been nominated as the democratic candidate for the House of Representatives in that State. This intelligence has been hailed with the highest satisfaction by his numerous friends here, whose earnest wishes for his future health and prosperity he bore with him in his departure last year.

Mr. C. was a resident among us for a period of seven years, during which time he earned himself an enviable distinction at the Bar of this place and of this Judicial circuit, as a sound and able lawyer, and as a citizen none could have been more esteemed. His honesty, integrity, and industry were worthy the imitation of all, whilst his unquestioned legal abilities reflected credit as well upon himself as upon the profession of which he was a member. Politically, Mr. C. was a prominent, active and radical democrat, never tiring in furthering the good cause. He has labored shoulder to shoulder with the democrats of old Seneca in the most trying times of the past, and we know they will ever be rejoiced to learn of his prosperity in his new home in "the far west."

The Dictator.

No ———— ever had so merciless a dis-

to Gen. Scott, we are ac with the reflection, that wh plaining of all others, he complain of nobody but hi

In our last we alluded to correspondence of Mr. M Scott. We showed that (manded his recall, and that which the federal press about the *persecution* of thi cer, was a mere *ruse de* Scott *demanded* his *recall*— surprised the War Dep took offence at the mission to negotiate a peace, and h quarrelled. Nor was the (fault, for the nicest precau ken to prevent a conflict of upon a review of those pre Marcy in his reply to Gen. 12, 1847 says, the "most sensitiveness could not pro slightest exception to the c pursued." Nor was the partial. If it was the in Government to supplant G missionary Mr. T. was ve ported, for Mr. Marcy say letter, "that while the Presi pelled to regard your (Gen. as the result of an entire the powers and duties of M grets to perceive that the co T., on the other hand, *has from error.*" Does this se accusation of Gen. Scott? G umbrage at the mission of without the slightest cause, President an impertinent an ful letter, demanding his re army, then engaged in ser Gen. Scott's position, as c

11

The Case against the Witnesses

The title of this chapter is the call of conflict, suggesting the excitement of debate and invincible proof. Similar titles used by anti-Mormon publications deliver this and no more. Argument is a poor tool for discovering truth because it defends a narrow position but usually lacks breadth. Anyone can make a "case" for or against anything. The right way to investigate is to gather comprehensively and then seek to understand. The opposite rule has been adopted for well over a hundred years as anti-Mormon books have downgraded the Book of Mormon witnesses. They typically ignore the great body of information from the witnesses themselves and instead concentrate on irregular statements from secondhand sources, adding liberal amounts of character assassination. But an array of half-truths presented in a combative manner should not satisfy a thinking person—in fact, many a conversion to Mormonism has started by shock at the obvious unfairness of such literature. Since these witnesses were trustworthy but not perfect they can be ridiculed by hypercritical methods, though they stand historically as honest men. But what of the attacks on their testimony of seeing the plates?

A main safeguard exists for testing claims that a witness modified his testimony—be sure that all statements come from the witness himself. Courts formalize this policy by various rules against hearsay, for one of the main questions about evidence is its directness, whether it is firsthand. David Whitmer complained in print that two encyclopedias published statements that he had denied his testimony, but his correction hardly solved the problem, for other editions and other books perpetuated that error.[1] In short, accurate evidence from a Book of Mormon witness must come from the witness—not from garbled reports through intermediaries. Almost all of the first generation of anti-Mormon writers ignored this basic rule, and now even educated authors may do no better. An example is the slanted biography of Joseph Smith by Fawn Brodie, who thought that "the three witnesses all told different versions of their experience" because she read this in "the local press of the time."[2] Her source is the heavily satirical *Palmyra Reflector,* and in describing it she indicated that "David Whitmer told the editor of the *Reflector*" a story of seeing the plates but no angel.[3] But these details are sloppy versions of what originally appeared, for the newspaper editor was not at all quoting David Whitmer, but "our informant," who seems not to have had any notes on his interview' since he "did not recollect precisely" the dimensions of the plates that David Whitmer reportedly gave.[4] So a verbal diagram of the source of this statement is: Brodie's version, of an editor's version, of his informant's version, of what David Whitmer said (not necessarily to the "informant"). If Brodie had quoted the article, that would have eliminated one stage of the hearsay, but instead she has furnished evidence at least three steps away from the Book of Mormon witness. In history the goal is to present the source itself, and not serve it dangerously spoiled by being warmed over several times.

Although we are discussing specific objections to Book of Mormon witnesses, the methods of response should be helpful in similar claims not discussed for lack of space. Most discrediting attempts use the inferior type of quotation illustrated above. If a supposed statement of a witness is not in his hand or printed by his authorization, the question becomes whether he was interviewed by a known individual attempting to report him accurately. Since we know some 200 specific individuals who fit these requirements, statements of indefinite origin from anonymous informants have no place. If the witnesses' words move down through a chain of individuals quoting others, the number of links must be evaluated—but above all the first link must be a trustworthy person who heard the witness. As an additional example, this principle is seriously violated by quoting a poem mentioning Oliver Cowdery in the Church newspaper at Nauvoo:

> Or prove the gospel was not true
>   Because old Paul the Saints could kill?
> Because the Jews its author slew
>   And now reject their Saviour still?
> Or prove that Christ was not the Lord
>   Because that Peter cursed and swore?
> Or Book of Mormon not his word
>   Because denied by Oliver?[5]

These are central stanzas of Joel H. Johnson's poem arguing that the restored gospel is true no matter who betrayed the cause. One must ask first what he specifically intended to say about Oliver, and then the exact source of his information. Before claiming that Johnson "admitted" Cowdery's denial of his testimony, one must assume that "denied" is used in the narrow sense of renouncing, and not in the more general sense of "setting aside" the Book of Mormon in practice, though passively knowing it true. For instance, it is popularly said that Peter "denied" Christ, one of Johnson's examples. In reality Peter did not deny Christ's divinity, for that was not in question—but he vehemently declined to be linked with Jesus at the high priest's house. Peter's "denial" by disassociating himself from Christ is parallel to Oliver's disassociation from the Book of Mormon by not actively promoting it for a time. This raises the larger question of whether Johnson as a poet intended to use narrow analytical language anyway, for his overstatement is evident in the cases of Paul killing Christians or the Jewish people killing Christ—neither is strictly true.

Thus one may take Johnson's poem too seriously by even asking where he got his information. But the poem has no evidential value, for when Oliver was excommunicated in Missouri in 1838, Johnson was still in Ohio and afterwards had no known contact with Cowdery. Johnson reviewed his life in this period in his short autobiography: "I helped to organize the Kirtland camp in 1838 and traveled with it as far as Springfield, Illinois; was called by council to stop there and take care of the sick. I commenced preaching and soon gathered a branch of the Church of forty members over which I presided until January 8, 1839, when the Lord showed me by revelation that I must immediately go to Carthage in Hancock County."[6] Since Johnson was not near Cowdery at excommunication or afterward, "denied by Oliver" is multiple hearsay at best. So after the objector takes one arbitrary meaning of "denied," he is left with Johnson quoting an unidentified number of middlemen, supposedly quoting Cowdery. It does not matter historically if an irresponsible rumor can be proved to be contemporary—it is still rumor without direct evidence to support it. When we ask for real contact with Cowdery, we find that Thomas B. Marsh questioned Oliver carefully right after he left the Church to find that he reaffirmed his Book of Mormon testimony at the height of his resentment against Joseph Smith.[7] This was quoted in the earlier chapter on Oliver's testimony, which also quoted Elizabeth Cowdery, who said that from 1829 to his death her husband "always without one doubt or shadow of turning affirmed the divinity and truth of the Book of Mormon."[8] Some people think that a wife would be biased, but from the strict angle of access to Oliver's attitude, who else would know better what he thought throughout his lifetime? Her statement that he never denied the Book of Mormon is made from the most direct and continuous experience possible.

The above hearsay situations raise the question of whether secondhand evidence started with observation. A related flaw is reporting only a part of what was first said. Lawyers insist on cross-examination to get the whole story, for a firsthand report of a half-truth is still misrepresentation. This kind of reporting occurs in a version of Martin Harris's speech by Stephen Burnett, writing at the height of his angry disillusionment with Joseph Smith.[9] His letter is contemporary, though heavily interpretive. Burnett stresses what he heard, but undoubtedly bends words to his theory:

> I have reflected long and deliberately upon the history of this church and weighed the evidence for and against it, loath to give it up. But when I came to hear Martin Harris state in public that he never saw the plates with his natural eyes, only in vision or imagination, neither Oliver nor David . . . the last pedestal gave way. . . . I therefore three weeks since in the Stone Chapel gave a full history of the Church since I became acquainted with it . . . I was followed by W. Parrish, Luke Johnson, and John Boynton, all of who concurred with me. After we were done speaking, M. Harris arose and said he was sorry for any man who rejected the Book of Mormon, for he knew it was true. He said that he had hefted the plates repeatedly in a box with only a tablecloth or a handkerchief over them, but he never

saw them, only as he saw a city through a mountain . . . For it is said on the 171 page of the Book of Covenants that the three should testify that they had seen the plates even as J.S. Jr., and if they only saw them spiritually or in vision with their eyes shut, J.S. Jr. never saw them in any other way—and if so the plates were only visionary.[10]

We are of course seeing Harris through the mind of a frustrated intermediary, one who thinks Mormonism presents a "whole scene of lying and deception."[11] He thinks that Martin Harris has not really seen the plates. If "only in vision," then Burnett (not Harris) says it was really just "imagination." If the Three Witnesses "only saw them spiritually," then Burnett (not Harris) can explain it as essentially "in vision with their eyes shut." But Martin Harris felt misrepresented, or he would not have stood up in the Kirtland Temple to challenge the explanations of Burnett and his disaffected associates. Note that there are two distinct experiences of Harris: (1) "he said that he had hefted the plates repeatedly in a box with only a tablecloth or handkerchief over them, but he never saw them, *only* as he saw a city through a mountain"; (2) "he never saw the plates with his natural eyes, *only* in vision." Getting at the real Martin Harris requires subtracting Burnett's sarcasm that seeps into the above wording. Note the two italicized appearances of *only* (italics added), used in the sense of *merely*, to say that besides lifting the box of plates Martin had also seen them "in vision," the point restated at the end of the quotation: "only saw them spiritually or in vision"; "only visionary." In other words, Burnett heard Martin say that he had seen the plates in vision, and when Burnett uses "only" four times to ridicule the experience, that shows his disbelief, not Martin's speech. Martin's candid denial of seeing the plates while translating was sometimes exaggerated into a denial of ever seeing the plates, but even Burnett reports Martin claiming two types of contact with the plates: lifting them thinly covered, plus later seeing them in the hands of the angel.[12] Some interviews add a third type of contact: handling the plates or turning their leaves. This probably happened long after the earliest experiences with the covered plates.

So Burnett paraphrased Martin Harris with the evident rationalizations of a skeptic. But Martin knew his own experience and remained a convinced Book of Mormon believer. Study of his interviews shows how strongly he insisted that the sight of the angel and plates was as real as the sight of the physical objects around him. His simple language in an 1870 letter is typical: "I do say that the angel did show to me the plates containing the Book of Mormon."[13] Here the "what" is more important than the "how." Martin saw the plates, his written testimony says, by means of the "marvelous" revelation of "an angel of God." Martin Harris never applied "only" to that experience. When Burnett says that the witness did not see "with his natural eyes," he fails to add that he still claimed vivid sight. John Gilbert, Book of Mormon typesetter, also remembered this kind of conversation: "I asked Harris once if he had really seen the plates with his naked eyes—his reply was 'No, but with spiritual eyes.' "[14] But the devout witness was confidently claiming something more, not something less than normal sight. Burnett represents Harris as equating his experience with that of David Whitmer and Oliver Cowdery. And as discussed, David rejected "either-or" by saying that he saw by both spiritual and natural means. The superb interview of Nathan Tanner, Jr. recorded David Whitmer's own words on this point: "He then explained that he saw the plates, and with his natural eyes, but he had to be prepared for it—that he and the other witnesses were overshadowed by the power of God and a halo of brightness indescribable."[15]

Oversimplification is distortion. Thus Burnett's report may be quite direct but lacks the second element in the courtroom oath: not only "tell the truth," but "the whole truth." Stephen Burnett's letter claims additional light on the Eight Witnesses, but there is a clear flaw in the source of his information. As discussed, Burnett heard original comments of Martin Harris, and then added that Martin Harris stood up later to refute the dissenters' interpretation of them. After mentioning "Oliver nor David" in the 1838 letter just quoted, Burnett continued his version of Harris's first talk: "and also that the eight witnesses never saw them and hesitated to sign that instrument for that reason, but were persuaded to do it." [16] When Martin attempted to correct this view of what he said, Burnett attributes this explanation to him: "and said he never should have told that the testimony of the eight was false, if it had not been picked out of him, but should have let it passed as it was." [17] What was really said? If Harris accused the bitter dissenters of twisting his first comments on the Eight Witnesses, can we trust them not to abuse his explanation? And what was the source of Harris's information anyway? No one claims he was quoting one of the Eight Witnesses. But we know that skeptical rumors thrived in the disbelieving climate at Kirtland, and Harris was probably alluding to one of those, most likely in disagreement. Burnett's letter is only one of several 1838 documents that clearly say that Martin would not give an inch on his testimony: "he was sorry for any man who rejected the Book of Mormon, for he knew it was true." Beyond Martin Harris, Burnett gives multiple hearsay from an unidentified source, and it has no value when the Eight Witnesses themselves contradict it consistently and clearly.

Unusual circumstances allowed one of the Eight Witnesses virtually to answer Burnett's letter of April, 1838. By May, Hyrum Smith had migrated from Ohio to Missouri, and on the way he visited Sally Parker, who in an August letter mentions how Warren Parrish and John Boynton were leading an apostate party of about thirty, many of whom denied the Book of Mormon.[18] Undoubtedly responding to these reports, Hyrum Smith had spoken in defense of the Book of Mormon, emphasizing that he was a witness because he knew by his physical senses. Sally wrote: "I have not heard but one sermon since we have been in the place, and that by Hyrum Smith. As he was moving to Missouri he tarried with us a little while. His discourse was beautiful. We was talking about the Book of Mormon, which he is one of the witnesses. He said he had but two hands and two eyes. He said he had seen the plates with his eyes and handled them with his hands." [19] There is no responsible report from any of the Eight Witnesses to the contrary. Their last survivor was John Whitmer, who was especially close to Hiram Page and the Whitmer brothers, all of whom left the Church. And John insisted, "I have never heard that any one of the three or eight witnesses ever denied the testimony that they have borne to the book, as published in the first edition of the Book of Mormon."[20] As discussed, both Hyrum Smith and John Whitmer published direct personal statements that they had "handled" the plates. That should settle Burnett's barb at the Eight Witnesses, for evidence is obviously better firsthand than thirdhand.

The above hearsay examples are like the party game of whispering a message around a circle—those who have played it realize that what starts through a series of individuals is often laughably garbled as the last version is announced. One put-down of the witnesses illustrates this embellishment of rumor. Governor Thomas Ford, whose administrative weakness contributed to the Prophet's death, retold a story that ought to have humor as its only serious purpose. Ford favored conspiracy to explain the Book of Mormon witnesses, but gave the alternate possibility of deluding the gullible, an epithet that really fits none of the men involved. In his words, "it is related" that the Prophet made faith the condition of seeing the plates, so after the witnesses had brainwashed themselves by fasting and intense desire, Joseph opened an empty box. After exclaiming, "Brother Joseph, we do not see the plates," they were answered with a tirade of divine threats unless they developed "a holy and living faith." Ford sketched two more hours of "fanatical" prayer, "at the end of which time, looking again into the box, they were now persuaded that they saw the plates."[21]

A good frontier yarn should be obvious, but this one continues to be used by people who might know better. Governor Ford said that it came from "men who were once in the confidence of the Prophet," no great recommendation of credibility for several Nauvoo braggarts of the stamp of John C. Bennett and Joseph H. Jackson. Thus hostile but anonymous informants are telling Ford what the Prophet supposedly said. Although Ford told the story about all witnesses, Harry Beardsley applied it only to the Three Witnesses and Fawn Brodie narrowed it to the Eight Witnesses.[22] She also upgrades the vague source—those "once in the confidence of the Prophet" are changed to "Joseph's key men." Thus Brodie gives this as "one of the most plausible descriptions of the manner in which Joseph Smith obtained these eight signatures," though that statement is contradicted when she finds it "difficult to reconcile this explanation" with the physical testimonies of the weight and dimensions of the plates.[23] Further "scholarly" use of this story appears in Edmund Wilson's anti-Mormon diatribe, based on Brodie's "documented and honest description" of the rise of Mormonism.[24] Wilson alludes to the Eight Witnesses' testimony of seeing and handling, "though they said that at first when the box was opened it had seemed to them to be empty till Smith had exhorted them to get down on their knees and pray for more faith."[25] So in educated folklore the original unidentified source gradually became the Eight Witnesses themselves, a result of Wilson quoting Brodie, Brodie quoting Ford, Ford quoting anonymous informants, with the story getting a little better at each retelling. If rationalism generates fictitious evolution in printed records, the careful student is well warned that skepticism, apostasy, and financial frustration went looking for theories of justification while the witnesses were still alive. To reiterate—the witnesses must speak by their own statements or those responsibly passed on through identified reporters.

True to debate tactics, even Brigham Young is used for the proposition that some official witnesses doubted their testimony. But a single sentence is usually quoted, not the full paragraph, in which Brigham specifically explains himself: "Some of the witnesses of the Book of Mormon who handled the plates and conversed with the angels of God, were afterwards left to doubt and to disbelieve that they had ever seen an angel. One of the Quorum of the Twelve, a young man full of faith and good works, prayed. And the vision of his mind was opened, and the angel of God came and laid the plates before him—and he saw and handled them, and saw the angel, and conversed with him as he would with one of his friends. But after all this, he was left to doubt, and plunged into apostasy, and has continued to contend against this work. There are hundreds in a similar condition."[26] Although the quotation is often associated with Oliver Cowdery, Brigham Young ruled him out of this situation: "Oliver Cowdery . . . never denied the Book of Mormon, not even in the wickedest days he ever saw."[27] But note whom Brigham has in mind—"a young man" who was a member of the "Quorum of the Twelve." None of the eleven whose names appear in the Book of Mormon were members of the council of apostles. Yet some others besides the eleven signers can also be called witnesses because they reported a vision similar to that received by the

Three Witnesses. For instance, Harrison Burgess wrote of an answer to prayer in 1833: "Suddenly a glorious personage clothed in white stood before me and exhibited to my view the plates from which the Book of Mormon was taken."[28] Martin Harris's wife had the same spectacular experience, though she violently rejected the restored gospel afterwards.[29] Other documented cases parallel these two.

So Brigham Young extended "witnesses of the Book of Mormon" beyond the normal reference to either the Three or the Eight Witnesses. John Taylor did also in an 1837 letter, speaking first of the Three Witnesses and their published testimony and adding, "Since that time angels have appeared to a great number of others, who bear testimony to the same things."[30] Who was in Brigham Young's mind as the doubting witness? The leading possibility is Luke Johnson, six years younger than Brigham and a member of the Twelve almost three years before his excommunication. A source to be quoted names him as a semi-witness of the Book of Mormon, saying that he even signed a statement, which cannot be verified. George A. Smith's 1838 letter from Kirtland names Luke Johnson as one who opposed the Book of Mormon among the dissenters, agreeing with some others "that it was nonsense."[31] But he repented and rejoined the Church in time to accompany the first pioneers to Utah, where he became a bishop. So he would fit Brigham Young's description if I "continued to contend against the work" referred to temporary apostasy. Anyway, the following 1846 experience of John D. Lee has striking parallels to Brigham Young's picture of the apostle-witness:

I went to St. Joseph, Mo. . . . While there I met Luke Johnson, one of the witnesses to the Book of Mormon. I had a curiosity to talk with him concerning the same. We took a walk down on the river bank. I asked him if the statement he signed about seeing the angel and the plates was true, if he did see the plates from which the Book of Mormon was printed or translated. He said it was true. I then said, "How is it that you have left the Church? if the angel appeared to you, and you saw the plates, how can you now live out of the Church? I understand you were one of the twelve apostles . . ." "I was one of the Twelve," said he; "I have not denied the truth of the Book of Mormon. But myself and several others were overtaken in a fault at Kirtland, Ohio. . . . I have come to the conclusion that each man is accountable for his own sins, also that the course I have been pursuing injures me alone, and I intend to visit the Saints and again ask to be admitted into the Church."[32]

The "case" against the Three Witnesses normally quotes some of their statements supposedly inconsistent with their testimony. Here the problem is not the truth of the statement as much as the logic of understanding it. For instance, in 1887 David Whitmer took special pains to print his religious position, his Address to all Believers in Christ, arguing that after being directed in the Book of Mormon and the early revelations, Joseph Smith added doctrines not of God, particularly plural marriage. David spent time on how wrong the Latter-day Saints were to excommunicate him, in the process claiming the following: "If you believe my testimony to the Book of Mormon; if you believe that God spake to us three witnesses by his own voice, then I tell you that in June, 1838, God spake to me again by his own voice from the heavens, and told me to 'separate myself from among the Latter-day Saints, for as they sought to do unto me, so should it be done unto them.' . . . I make no farther statements now, but suffice it to say that my persecutions, for trying to show them their errors became of such a nature that I had to leave the Latter Day Saints. And as I rode on horseback out of Far West in June, 1838, the voice of God from heaven spake to me as I have stated above."[33] These circumstances are well known to Mormon historians; after the excommunications of Oliver Cowdery and David and John Whitmer, Sidney Rigdon had

preached his "Salt Sermon," warning dissenters not to inter-
fere with Mormon society. The Whitmers and Cowdery were
next told to get out of town, and with turmoil caused by
forcible rejection, they left the Mormon center of Far West.
Joseph Smith and the Twelve later criticized Sidney Rigdon's
aggressive speeches and also the secret threatenings of
Sampson Avard, probably the chief mover in this expulsion.
What kind of a "voice" did David hear then? David does not
really say; he only implies that it was audible by comparing it
with the command to testify of the Book of Mormon.[34] But
there are problems with that because David Whitmer did not
treat the two experiences equally in his long lifetime. He only
mentioned the undefined voice at Far West once, in this last
writing to fellow believers—but he had repeatedly testified of
an audible voice authenticating the Book of Mormon.[35] Those
with him in 1830 in the New York grove certified that they had
also heard God's voice then, but neither Oliver Cowdery nor
John Whitmer, both of whom left Far West with David at this
time, say anything about the heavenly command of 1838.
Whatever came to David Whitmer, the later experience fails to
contradict his earlier divine command to testify of the ancient
record. David Whitmer could have received true spiritual
comfort because of the unjust methods that his former associates were using against him; or he may have only felt that God
spoke to him because of the powerful indignation that swelled
up in his soul; or if he gave way to the spirit of anger and
retaliation, he invited Satan to inspire him and deceive him.
For instance, once in later life he was tempted to lead, thereby
dictating several revelations that he later considered false.[36]
The Far West "voice" might fall into this category.

Studying a problem with a Book of Mormon witness will
generally lead to better understanding of the witness, the situation with an 1844 report: "Martin Harris is a firm believer

in Shakerism, says his testimony is greater than it was of the Book of Mormon."[37] This word to the Twelve from Phineas Young and others is vague, for we do not know whether these Kirtland Mormons heard Martin Harris say this, or whether they heard it secondhand. His leaning to Shakerism is probably accurate, but Harris's precise wording is all-important if one claims that he testified of Shakerism instead of the Book of Mormon. This "either-or" reading of the document does not fit Martin's lifetime summary of all his interviews: "no man ever heard me in any way deny the truth of the Book of Mormon, the administration of the angel that showed me the plates."[38] For instance, at the same time as the above 1844 letter, Edward Bunker met Martin in the Kirtland Temple, visited his home, "and heard him bear his testimony to the truth of the Book of Mormon."[39] And six months later Jeremiah Cooper traveled to Kirtland and visited with Martin Harris: "he bore testimony to the truth of the Book of Mormon."[40]

Martin's Shaker sympathies terminated some time before 1855, when Thomas Colburn reported his attitude: "he tried the Shakers, but that would not do."[41] In the meantime Martin was intrigued by their claims of revelation, though he surely never espoused all Shaker beliefs, for thoroughgoing Shakers renounced the married life that Martin had during these years.[42] Fully committed Shakers also lived in communities like nearby North Union, whereas Martin remained in Kirtland during this period. Their appeal lay in a Pentecostal seeking of the Spirit and emphasis on preparation for Christ's coming. When Phineas Young mentioned Martin's Shaker belief, a new book of Shaker origin was circulating, "A Holy, Sacred, and Divine Roll and Book, from the Lord God of Heaven to the Inhabitants of Earth." Since it claimed to come from angels to prepare the world for the Millennium, it would be broadly harmonious with Martin Harris's commitment to the Book of Mormon, which in a far more historical and rational sense is committed to the same goal. Indeed, the Shaker movement later tended to slough off the "Divine Roll" as produced by an excess of enthusiasm.[43] We do not know whether Martin ever accepted this book as true, but he showed one like it to a visitor. This act does not show belief in that book, since it may have been exhibited as a curiosity, but the following journal entry shows that even if Shaker literature was present in 1850, Martin still gave priority to his Book of Mormon testimony: "I went to see Martin Harris. He was one of the 3 Witnesses to the Book of Mormon and said he knew it was true, for he saw the plates and knew for himself. I heard his little girl—she was 7 years old. I read some in what they called the Holy Roll, but no God."[44] Anyone following this discussion can soon see that authentic statements from the Book of Mormon witnesses are voluminous and always repeat the reality of their experience. Yet the first anti-Mormon book was written in 1834 within a dozen miles of their residences and set the precedent of not contacting them but devoting most space to show them to be either superstitious or dishonest.[45] This became a formula: ignore the testimony and attack the witness, the same pattern as the detailed current treatments. That method is sure to caricature its victims: lead off with the worst names anyone ever called them, take all charges as presented without investigating, solidify mistakes as lifelong characteristics, and ignore all positive accomplishments or favorable judgments on their lives. Such bad methods will inevitably produce bad men on paper. The only problem with this treatment is that it cheats the consumer—it appears to investigate personality without really doing so. A few central examples are in order.

David Whitmer is attacked because he allowed William E. McLellin to appoint him president of a reorganized church in

1848, after which David received some revelations. It was an easy decision for David; praying beforehand "his whole frame trembled and shook . . . and he cried out, 'Brethren, lay hands upon me that I may have strength to do my duty.'"[46] Some months afterward David directed a letter explaining that his actions were not proper and had been made "after three days successive intreaties."[47] Prior to the 1835 appointment of the Twelve, David Whitmer had been set apart as the successor to Joseph, but he did not use this precedent for personal aggrandizement. The above false start was four years after Joseph's death; it was followed years later by David's Small Church of Christ that claimed the identical organization of 1829–30 while Joseph Smith was at the Whitmer home in New York. William E. McLellin's later letters show constant pressure to reinterest David in a presidency over a reorganized church, which David steadfastly declined. In fifty years out of the Church the main theme of David's career is conservatism and not advancing beyond the first revelations of the Restoration. This reality is virtually the opposite of the "credulous" term currently applied to David. David was in fact religiously opinionated rather than religiously unstable. This witness obviously hoped to be active again in the Church after Joseph's death, so his major miscalculation about his own leadership authority had its own logic at that time. Searching honestly and admitting failure is hardly a moral blot—at least anyone who has seriously investigated other beliefs or changed churches should not think so.

Martin Harris displays a certain instability not at all characteristic of David Whitmer and Oliver Cowdery, but his lifetime religious positions have a consistency that is clear because of remarkable information from him. As discussed, the Book of Mormon remained the mainstay of a life that was repeatedly confused by the loss of family, wealth, friends, and religious security. His decision to oppose Joseph Smith in Kirtland led him into a series of theological adaptations; eight of them brought him back the full circle to rejoin the Latter-day Saints in the West. This figure has been seized upon for condemnation rather than insight. Furthermore, one early source claims that Martin went through five religious positions before becoming a Mormon, so the "case" against the witnesses adds eight and five to exclaim in shock that Martin made thirteen changes. But this ignores my specific explanations of the eight changes after his 1838 excommunication: except for Shakerism, "every affiliation of Martin Harris was with some Mormon group."[48] Beginning algebra teachers caution against adding eight oranges and five apples—the answer is not thirteen because the categories do not mix.

We shall see that the "five changes" prior to Martin's New York conversion are overstated—but differing churches of that period do not mix with Martin's Ohio variations on Mormonism, which he told visitors he had never left. His specific Ohio stages include the following: (1) the Parrish-Boynton party (which he condemned for denying the Book of Mormon at the time he met with them); (2) an 1842 rebaptism by a Nauvoo missionary; (3) an 1846 English mission with a Strangite companion (where documents suggest that the Book of Mormon was really Martin's message); (4) participation in McLellin's attempts to set up Midwest leaders for the Church in 1847–48; (5) concurrent with one or more stages, sympathy for Shakerism without full participation; (6) support of Gladden Bishop in his program of further revelations based on the Book of Mormon; (7) continuation of his original "dissenter" status of stressing the Book of Mormon and early revelations of Joseph Smith—even when occasionally meeting with William Smith and others, he maintained this position for fifteen years after his 1855 conversations with

Thomas Colburn; (8) his 1870 return to the Church in Salt Lake. Note that the emphasis could be on the number "eight" or Martin's support of the Book of Mormon through all stages, which blended as different ways of trying to further the Restoration.

The arithmetic of Martin's five religious changes before Mormonism is also faulty. The claim comes from the hostile Palmyra affidavits published by E. D. Howe; G. W. Stoddard closed his in sarcasm against Martin Harris: "He was first an orthodox Quaker, then a Universalist, next a Restorationer, then a Baptist, next a Presbyterian, and then a Mormon."[49] Palmyra sources do not yet prove that Martin was a Quaker, though his wife probably was.[50] And no evidence yet associates Martin with the Baptist or Presbyterian churches. Note that the other two names are religious positions, not necessarily churches—philosophical Universalists dissent from traditional churches in believing that God will save all, and Restorationists obviously take literally the many Bible prophecies of God's reestablished work in modern times. An early Episcopal minister in Palmyra interviewed Martin and reduced his five positions to two: "He had been, if I mistake not, at one period a member of the Methodist Church, and subsequently had identified himself with the Universalists."[51] Of course Martin could have been a Universalist and Restorationer simultaneously. This view fits what other Palmyra sources say about Martin Harris. In the slanted words of Pomeroy Tucker, who knew him personally, "He was a religious monomaniac, reading the Scriptures intently, and could probably repeat from memory nearly every text of the Bible from beginning to end, chapter and verse in each case."[52]

This impression of Martin as Bible student outside of organized religions is just what Martin says in his little-known autobiography of this period:

In the year 1818–52 years ago—I was inspired of the Lord and taught of the Spirit that I should not join any church, although I was anxiously sought for by many of the sectarians. I was taught two could not walk together unless agreed. What can you not be agreed [is] in the Trinity because I cannot find it in my Bible, Find it for me, and I am ready to receive it. . . . Others' sects, the Episcopalians, also tried me—they say 3 persons in one God, without body, parts, or passions. I told them such a God I would not be afraid of: I could not please or offend him. . . . The Methodists took their creed from me. I told them to release it or I would sue them . . . The Spirit told me to join none of the churches, for none had authority from the Lord, for there will not be a true church on the earth until the words of Isaiah shall be fulfilled. . . . So I remained until the Church was organized by Joseph Smith the Prophet. Then I was baptized . . . being the first after Joseph and Oliver Cowdery. And then the Spirit bore testimony that this was all right, and I rejoiced in the established Church. Previous to my being baptized I became a witness of the plates of the Book of Mormon.[53]

The above is Martin Harris's creed, held for the half-century before giving this statement on returning to the Church, plus the five additional years that he lived in Utah. For the dozen years prior to joining Mormonism he was a seeker, like scores of other LIDS converts, and through life never departed from his confidence that the Bible prophecies were fulfilled in the Restoration through Joseph Smith. This core belief was what everything else related to, the structure that stood before, during, and after any gingerbread decorations at Kirtland.

The purpose here is not to win arguments but bring greater understanding of each main Book of Mormon witness. Oliver Cowdery's inner feelings expressed in his letters out of the Church throw more light on his character than a study of the meaning of overdone accusations after his excommunication. Oliver's letters insisted that these charges were false, and the same writings show what he considered true in the

Church. Five years after leaving Far West Oliver answered the Twelve, saying that he felt "sensibly and keenly" about correcting the "falsehoods" in print.[54] Then his letter extended warmth to his former priesthood brethren, sharing faith that his professional success had come through the Lord's blessing: "I only speak of it here to express the gratitude of my own heart to the Lord our Common Father, who has thus enabled me to provide support for a destitute family."[55] Above all he expressed brotherhood with the apostles that eight years before had been selected by the Three Witnesses in council with the Prophet—the apostles who had been given a moving charge by Oliver, who had then exhorted them to seek direct revelations from God, after which Oliver took each apostle by the hand to ask if he would accept the responsibility of the ordination just conferred.[56] His 1843 letter reexpressed confidence in the authority of those men "who once took me by the hand, under the sanction of the Holy Spirit, when they received a high and holy calling."[57]

Such language contrasts with the threadbare patchwork of a supposed 1839 pamphlet from this Book of Mormon witness, who in the Church spoke and wrote about receiving priesthood restoration from John the Baptist and later from the ancient apostles Peter, James, and John.[58] This pamphlet is confused in saying that he is "beginning to doubt" the priesthood, and adding that the voice of John the Baptist "did most mysteriously resemble the voice of Elder Sidney Rigdon." Yet it adds nothing about the great apostolic visitation that Oliver generally mentioned in his priesthood restoration narratives. The suspect pamphlet closes with a convenient revelation of the Savior himself, wherein "the Redeemer instructed me plainly" that Joseph Smith had falsely introduced "high priests, apostles, and other officers" into the Church. If Oliver

171

had really received this revelation in 1839, he would not have referred to the "high and holy calling" of the Twelve in the above letter in 1843.

What the real Oliver Cowdery was saying out of the Church about the ministry of angels does not appear in this production, titled *Defense in a Rehearsal of My Grounds for Separating Myself from the Latter Day Saints* (Norton, Ohio, 1839). Not only does Cowdery have no 1839 connection with the place of publication; not only does the supposed location have no known press—but also no known original of this pamphlet has been found.[59] It came from an anti-Mormon organization in 1906 with the fanfare of new discovery, but was totally unmentioned in Oliver Cowdery's lifetime in Mormon publications (which typically refuted attacks in this period) or non-Mormon publications (which would not have passed up the printed renunciation of the key assistant to Joseph Smith).[60] Furthermore, when Oliver returned to the Church and was closely questioned on what he had published about Mormonism while out of the Church, the above item was not ever named.

The spirit of conviction of Oliver Cowdery's own language was reiterated in an 1846 letter to Oliver's brother-in-law, Phineas Young. Speaking privately and spontaneously, Oliver tied his personal integrity to his priesthood restoration testimony, one that stands on the same ground as his similar Book of Mormon testimony. In pleading that the printed record be set straight before his return to the Church, Oliver spoke pointed words applicable to anyone repeating the unsubstantiated libels to which he refers:

And that I may not be misunderstood, let me here say that I have only sought and only asked that my character might stand exonerated from those charges which imputed to me the crimes of theft, forgery, etc.—those which all my former associates knew to be false. I do not, I have never asked to be excused or exempted from an acknowledgment of any actual fault or wrong, for of these there are many, which it always was my pleasure to confess. I have cherished a hope, and that one of my fondest, that I might leave such a character, as to those who might believe in my testimony after I should be called hence, might do so, not only for the sake of the truth, but might not *blush* for the private character of the man who bore that testimony. I have been sensitive on this subject I admit, but I ought to be so. You would be under the circumstances, had you stood in the presence of John, with our departed Brother Joseph, to receive the Lesser Priesthood, and in the presence of Peter, to receive the Greater, and looked down through time, and witnessed the effects these two must produce. You would feel what you have never felt, were wicked men conspiring to lessen the effects of your testimony on man after you should have gone to your long sought rest. [61]

The above letter is Oliver's disagreement with the most quoted document used against his character. That is the purported ultimatum directed to David Whitmer and Oliver Cowdery causing them to leave Far West—but Oliver's 1843 letter to the Twelve refers to its published form and suggests that he had never seen such a document.[62] It was published by the State of Missouri as part of Joseph Smith's commitment hearing, which contained only the prosecution's case. The ultimatum was incorporated in the testimony of Sampson Avard, the most disreputable Mormon apostate on record, and his name headed the list of "signers," making it very possible that he wrote the document and filled it with exaggerations.[63] Even if the document is authentic, the Book of Mormon witnesses fled immediately and were not allowed to respond. Quoting it as evidence against the Cowdery and Whitmer character (with some books carelessly adding Martin Harris, who was not even in Missouri) only proves that "a little learning is a dangerous thing"—dangerous especially to the reputations of men victimized by one-sided use of one-sided documents divorced from their context.

Two months earlier Cowdery was invited to answer charges at his excommunication, though he chose only to write a letter about three charges, which were dropped. The six remaining charges were for inactivity in the Church, for speaking against Joseph Smith, and for seeking to collect money from an impoverished people through lawsuits. This much was proved at the trial and by independent historical records of Oliver's activities then, including his personal letters to his relatives just before excommunication. But one count was added that is doubtful both by the wording of the high council's charge and its findings: "For disgracing the Church by being connected in the 'bogus' business, as common report says."[64] Attributing this to "common report" is simply saying "hearsay," raising a special caution, reinforced by very vague and ambiguous testimony at the trial on this point. In fact, the other five findings against Oliver were unqualified, though this "8th charge was sustained satisfactorily by circumstantial evidence," another way of saying that solid proof was lacking.[65]

Fortunately for accurate history, every excommunicated Mormon is consulted again at reentrance to the Church, and the issue is inevitably whether the actions that caused excommunication have been remedied. This opportunity for a second look at the real problems of Oliver Cowdery came as the witness returned to the Church in Iowa in 1848, gave his public testimony, and then requested rebaptism from apostles, who referred his case to the high council and high priests quorum. A careful record was kept of the joint meeting, which raised no question about Oliver's honesty, always a requirement for baptism and rebaptism. Instead, Oliver's examination was specifically on not following priesthood leaders on Church issues: "many questions were relative to his course and feelings towards Brother Joseph Smith, etc."[66] This worthiness hearing not only clarified what the real problems were at the earlier excommunication but gave Oliver Cowdery the opportunity to state that he knew that his life had been virtuous: "I feel that I can honorably return. I have sustained an honorable character before the world during my absence from you. This though a small matter with you, is of vast importance."[67] This again reveals the spirit of the man who chose hard roads of conscience over popularity in his major conflicts of life. In the manner of his differing personality, each witness did the same. The moral merits of the Book of Mormon witnesses are all the stronger for serious investigation.

NOTES

1. David Whitmer, *An Address to All Believers in Christ* (Richmond, Mo., 1887), p. 8. An illustration is the scholarly *Catholic Encyclopedia* of 1913 (10:570), which mentioned the witnesses' printed testimonies and added this notable faux pas: "On renouncing Mormonism subsequently, Cowdery, Whitmer, and Harris, the three principal witnesses, declared this testimony false." The statement apparently depends on language of the *Encyclopaedia Britannica* that David Whitmer complained about.

2. Fawn M. Brodie, *No Man Knows My History* (New York: Alfred A. Knopf, 1946), pp. 77–78.

3. Ibid., p. 78 (cp. bottom notes, 77–78).

4. *The Reflector* (Palmyra, New York), Mar. 19, 1831, p. 126.

5. *Times and Seasons* 2 (1841):482.

6. Joel H. Johnson, Autobiography, *Utah Genealogical and Historical Magazine* 29 (1938):170–71. For the contemporary summary of these movements, see the February 6, 1840 letter of Johnson in *Times and Seasons* 1 (1840):76–77.

7. "History of Thomas Baldwin Marsh," Nov. 1857, also cit. *Deseret News,* Mar. 24, 1858.

8. Elizabeth Cowdery to David Whitmer, Mar. 8, 1887, cit. *The Return,* Dec. 1892, p. 9, with "shudder" corrected to "shadow."

9. Stephen Burnett appears in journals and minute entries as an early Ohio convert who served the Church with some ability until the economic trials of 1837 soured him. This conclusion is largely drawn from the letter quoted hereafter in the text, which spends as much time on financial losses as theological differences, and shows considerable bitterness at Joseph Smith for taking "the monies of the Church from their pockets and brought them nigh unto destruction." (S. Burnett to Lyman E. Johnson, Apr. 15, 1838, Orange Twonship, Geauga Co., Ohio, cit. Joseph Smith Letter Book 1:64–66.) Joseph's version of his difficulties was that Burnett "could not bear to have his purse taxed," so he "proclaimed all revelation lies." (Elders' Journal 1 [1838]:57.) The reference to "the 171 page of the Book of Covenants" refers to what is now D&C 17 in the 1835 edition of the Doctrine and Covenants. Cp. ch. 1, n. 16.

10. S. Burnett to Lyman E. Johnson, Apr. 15, 1838, Orange Township, Geauga Co., Ohio, cit. Joseph Smith Letter Book 1: 64–66.

11. Ibid.

12. Since Harris had physical experience with the covered plates in addition to the vision, one of the early and most quoted Harris interviews apparently merges the two experiences and claims a contradiction. Harris supposedly said of the plates, "I saw them just as distinctly as I see anything around me, though at the time they were covered with a cloth." This is not a direct Harris interview, but instead is John A. Clark's version of the version of "a gentleman in Palmyra" who talked to Harris. *Gleanings By the Way* (New York, 1842), pp. 256–57.

13. Martin Harris to Mr. Emerson (Hanna B. Emerson), Nov. 23, 1870, Smithfield, Utah, cit. *True Latter Day Saints' Herald* 22 (1875):630.

14. John H. Gilbert to James T. Cobb, Mar. 16, 1879, Palmyra, N.Y., manuscript at New York Public Library.

15. Nathan Tanner, Jr., Journal, Apr. 13, 1886.

16. Burnett to Johnson.

17. Ibid.

18. Hyrum's move is dated by his journal volume in the hands of Elder Eldred G. Smith: "Arrived in the Far West May 29, 1838." Cp. Mercy Fielding Thompson's recollections in her family letter of Dec. 20, 1880: "We remained there [Canada] until March, 1838, when we were appointed to journey with Hyrum Smith . . . to Far West, Missouri. We arrived there in May, where my daughter Mary Jane was born on the 14th of June, 1838." Also cit. Don C. Corbett, *Mary Fielding Smith* (Salt Lake City: Deseret Book Co., 1970), p. 52. Cp. Hyrum Smith's affidavit regarding Missouri: "I left Kirtland, Ohio, in the spring of 1838, having the charge of a family of ten individuals." *History of the Church* 3:373.

19. Sally Parker to Francis Tufts, Aug. 26, 1838, evidently written at Sunbury, Ohio, but posted at Kirtland Mills. Manuscript is in possession of a descendant.

20. John Whitmer to Mark H. Forest [Forscutt], Mar. 5, 1876, signed handscript at RLDS Archives, Independence, Mo. Cp. William Smith's similar evaluation of all of the witnesses, with his special knowledge of the Smiths: "nor has either or any one of these witnesses ever to my knowledge counteracted the testimony as given above concerning the real existence of these Mormon tablets." Notes written on "Chambers' Life of Joseph Smith," typescript, pp. 8–9.

21. Thomas Ford, *History of Illinois* (Chicago, 1854), p. 257.

22. Harry M. Beardsley, *Joseph Smith and His Mormon Empire* (Boston, 1931), p. 67; Brodie, p. 79.

23. Ibid., pp. 79–80.

24. Edmund Wilson, *The Dead Sea Scrolls, 1947–1969* (New York: Oxford University Press, 1969), p. 279.

25. Ibid., p. 284.

26. *Journal of Discourses* 7:164.

27. JD 2:257. Cp. Brigham Young's 1870 October Conference address: "Oliver Cowdery . . . always maintained his first testimony that God has sent an

angel and revealed to him that the book was true"—a concept on this occasion applied specifically to Martin Harris and by strong implication to David Whitmer. (*Ogden Junction,* Oct. 12, 1870.)

28. Harrison Burgess, "Sketch of a Well-spent Life," cit. *Labor in the Vineyard* (Salt Lake City, 1884), p. 66.

29. *Biographical Sketches,* p. 112.

30. John Taylor to "Rev. and Dear Sir," May 3, 1837, cit. *Latter Day Saints' Messenger and Advocate* 3 (1837):513.

31. George A. Smith to Josiah Fleming, Mar. 30, 1838. How much Luke Johnson doubted the Book of Mormon is not known, since Eliza R. Snow pictured him as "jovial" and "more inclined to ridicule than hostility." *Biography and Family Record of Lorenzo Snow* (Salt Lake City, 1884). In addition to Luke, another possibility is his brother and apostle Lyman Johnson, whom Lorenzo Snow pictured as seeing an angel but being overcome by Satan afterward. See Mathias F. Cowley, Conference Report, Oct., 1901, p. 18, suggested by researcher E. Jay Bell.

32. John D. Lee, *Mormonism Unveiled* (Saint Louis, 1877), p. 184.

33. David Whitmer, *Address to All Believers in Christ,* pp. 27–28.

34. For the caution that the 1838 "voice of God" might be the "voice of the Spirit," compare the following statements. Speaking prospectively of the Address that he would publish, David said: "Now God has made it known to me that before I go hence, I must send forth my testimony to the world." (David Whitmer to Joseph Smith III, Dec. 9, 1886, cit. *Saints' Herald* 34 [1887]:89.) David later made clear that the above revelation came from the Spirit: "But now the Spirit of God has made it manifest to me to make them known." (*Address to All Believers in Christ,* p. 25.)

35. For the definition of the 1830 voice as distinctly heard and shared by the senses, see the following. "I . . . distinctly heard the voice of the Lord declaiming that the records of the plates of the Book of Mormon were translated by the gift and power of God." (*Kansas City Journal,* June 5, 1881.) "I heard the voice of the Lord as distinctly as I ever heard anything in my life declaring that they (the plates) were translated by the gift and power of God." Joseph F. Smith, journal, Sept. 8, 1878, cit. Joseph Fielding Smith, *Life of Joseph F. Smith* (Salt Lake City, 1938), p. 243.

36. David called these revelations "errors in doctrine in the past." (*Address to All Believers in Christ,* p. 28.) See the discussion on pages 166–67 of this chapter.

37. Phineas Young et al. to "Beloved Brethren" who in the last of the letter are defined as "our brethren, the Twelve," Dec. 31, 1844, Kirtland, Ohio.

38. Martin Harris, Sr., to H. Emerson, Jan., 1871, Smithfield, Utah, cit. *True Latter Day Saints' Herald* 22 (1875):630.

39. Edward Bunker, Autobiography, manuscript, p. 3.

40. Jeremiah Cooper to E. Robinson, Sept. 3, 1845, cit. *Messenger and Advocate of the Church of Christ* 1 (1845):319.

41. Thomas Colburn to Elder Snow, May 2, 1855, cit. *St. Louis Luminary,* May 5, 1855.

42. Martin remarried Caroline Young before his estrangement from the Church and had children in the years 1838, 1842, 1845, 1849, 1854, and 1856.

43. For a survey of the rise and fall of the 1843 "Divine Roll," see Charles Nordhoff, *Communistic Societies of the United States* (New York, 1874), pp. 245–50.

44. James Willard Bay, Journal, Nov. 23, 1850, p. 27.

45. E. D. Howe, *Mormonism Unvailed* (Painesville, Ohio, 1834), pp. 96–99.

46. *Ensign of Liberty* 1 (1849):99–100.

47. Hiram Page to Alfred Bonny et al., June 24, 1849, Richmond, Mo., answering "a letter directed to David Whitener," *Olive Branch* 2 (1849):28–29.

48. First printed as Richard Lloyd Anderson, "The Certainty of the Skeptical Witness," *Improvement Era*, Mar., 1969, p. 63.

49. Howe, *Mormonism Unvailed*, p. 261.

50. See Pomeroy Tucker, *Origin, Rise, and Progress of Mormonism* (New York, 1867), P. 41.

51. John A. Clark, *Episcopal Recorder* 18 (1840):94.

52. Tucker, *Mormonism*, p. 52.

53. Testimony of Martin Harris, dictated to Edward Stevenson, Sept. 4, 1870, Stevenson microfilm collection, after journal, vol. 32. Researchers are greatly indebted to descendant Joseph Grant Stevenson for locating and publishing this document in the *Stevenson Family History* (Provo, Utah: Stevenson Publishing Co., 1955), 1:163–64. Appreciation also goes to Max Parkin for reminding me of the item, no. 1043 in Davis Bitton, *Guide to Mormon Diaries and Autobiographies* (Provo, Utah: Brigham Young University Press, 1977), p. 146. My text follows my rereading of the microfilm. Martin's view of being baptized right after the first two elders probably refers to events of April 6, 1830.

54. Oliver Cowdery to the Twelve, Dec. 25, 1843, Tiffin, Ohio.

55. Ibid.

56. See HC 2:194–98.

57. Cowdery to the Twelve, Dec. 25, 1843.

58. See Richard Lloyd Anderson, "The Second Witness of Priesthood Restoration," *Improvement Era*, Sept., 1968, pp. 14–24.

59. See Chad J. Flake, *Mormon Bibliography, 1830–1930* (Salt Lake City: University of Utah Press, 1978), p. 182 (item 2544): "All copies are photostat. . . . Whether the pamphlet ever existed is doubtful." Cp. the annotation on Neal's 1906 first publication (p. 455, item 5744): "This is the version from which all copies have been taken."

60. The first known appearance of this item attributed to Cowdery is R. B. Neal, *Oliver Cowdery's Defense and Renunciation* (Ashland, Ky., 1906). Neal was the general secretary of the American Anti-Mormon Association and claimed to discover the pamphlet, though never disclosing where or even discussing its authenticity. In his first printing, he mentions John the Revelator's continuing priesthood, saying, "We made the same argument years ago that Oliver here makes" (p. 15).

61. Oliver Cowdery to Phineas Young, Mar. 23, 1846, Tiffin, Ohio. The letter is transcribed quite accurately in Stanley R. Gunn, *Oliver Cowdery* (Salt Lake City: Bookcraft, 1962), pp. 250–51.

62. See Cowdery to the Twelve, Dec. 25, 1843: "I cannot speak definitely of

this instrument, as I know nothing of it except what has been related by those who say they have seen it."

63. See Sampson Avard et al. to Oliver Cowdery et al., June, 1838, Far West, cit. *Document Containing the Correspondence, Orders, etc. in Relation to the Disturbances with the Mormons* (Fayette, Mo., 1841), pp. 103–6. This Avard ultimatum is regularly cited without mentioning that it is part of the Sampson Avard testimony, a misleading impression of official approval of a strictly ex parte hearing, in which each piece of evidence has to be judged according to its source. There are serious historical problems in Avard's testimony. For instance, the other document he quoted in addition to the witnesses' ultimatum is the "secret constitution" of the Danite group, but dissenter John Corrill concluded "that but few knew about it, for I never heard one lisp on the subject until Avard exposed it after he was arrested." *Brief History of the Church of Christ of Latter Day Saints* (Saint Louis, 1839), p. 32. Avard claimed that Sidney Rigdon penned the 'witnesses' ultimatum, but Avard could have invented both documents to produce impressive testimony for his own benefit.

64. Far West Record, p. 119, where quotation marks appear around "bogus," also cit. HC 3:16.

65. Far West Record, p. 126. The precise wording of the finding was lost in the summary made in HC 3:17.

66. Pottawattamie High Council Minutes, Nov. 5, 1848. For the discussion then on Oliver's views of the priesthood while out of the Church, see Richard Lloyd Anderson, "The Second Witness on Priesthood Succession," *Improvement Era*, Nov., 1968, pp. 14–20.

67. Pottawattamie High Council Minutes, Nov. 5, 1848.

Angel with plates, Hill Cumorah Monument. (Statue by Torlief Knaphus).

12

The Challenge
of the Witnesses

Historians collect facts and then evaluate facts. Law courts separate the functions of establishing facts from judging facts, the latter of which is often left to a jury. This study of the Book of Mormon witnesses used strictest historical standards in recovering information—everything possible on their lives and testimonies, sparing no expense or trouble. These materials have been classified, correlated, and tested on the basis of their firsthand value. Statements clearly traced to the witnesses verify the testimonies printed in the Book of Mormon that they saw the plates, and in the case of the Three Witnesses, that an angel displayed them while the heavenly voice declared that the translation was correct. Thus historical tools show that a dozen men (Joseph Smith and all eleven witnesses) repeated the above story with conviction over their lifetimes. They occasionally witnessed to other spiritual experiences supplementing the above, but at no known time did any Book of Mormon witness retract his printed testimony. The first Mormons knew the witnesses and kept track of them through reliable reports—and always insisted that none modified his testimony. For instance, Orson Pratt visited most of the witnesses in New York within months after the publication of the Book of Mormon. He met with them continually prior to their excommunications, and in the perspective of nearly half a century reviewed his personal knowledge and investigation of the Three Witnesses.

Now did either of these three men . . . ever in any way deny the divinity of the Book of Mormon? Never, no never. Whatever the circumstances they were placed in, however much they were mobbed and ridiculed, however much they suffered by the persecution of their enemies, their testimony all the time was—"We saw the angel of God, we beheld him in his glory, we saw the plates in his hands, and the engravings thereon, and we know that the Book of Mormon is true." . . .

Oliver Cowdery did not live his faith as he should have done, and he was excommunicated from this Church during Joseph's lifetime. Did he still continue to hold fast to his testimony? He did. Never was he known to swerve from it in the least degree. And after being out of the Church several years, he returned to Council Bluffs, where there was a branch of the Church, and at a conference he acknowledged his sins and humbly asked the Church to forgive him, bearing his testimony to the sacred things recorded in the Book of Mormon—that he saw the angel and the plates, just according to the testimony to which he had appended his name. He was rebaptized a member of the Church, and soon after departed this life.

Martin Harris did not follow up this people in the State of Missouri; neither did he follow us up to the State of Illinois. But we often heard of him telling in public and in private of the great vision that God had shown to him concerning the divinity of the Book of Mormon. A few years ago he came to this Territory, an old man, between eighty and ninety years of age, and spoke from this stand in the hearing of the people. He then located himself in Cache county, in the northern part of the Territory, where he continued to live until last Saturday, when he departed this life in his ninety-third year—a good old age. Did he continue to bear testimony all that length of time—over forty-six years of his life? Did he at any time during that long period waver in the least degree from his testimony? Not at all. He had a great many follies and imperfections, like all other people, like the ancient apostles, like Elijah the Prophet, but after all, he continued to testify to the very last concerning the truth of this work. . . .

182

As I have already mentioned, one more witness remains who saw that angel and the plates. Who is it? David Whitmer, a younger man than Martin Harris . . . Where does he live? In the western part of Missouri. Does he still hold fast to his testimony? He does. Many of the elders of this Church, in going to and fro among the nations, have called upon him from time to time, and they all bear the same testimony—that Mr. David Whitmer still, in the most solemn manner, declares that he saw the angel and that he saw the plates in his hands.[1]

Since these facts are clear, the only serious question about the Book of Mormon witnesses is not what their testimony was, but how to evaluate it. History cannot change their words, which by itself is impressive, for religion has attracted its share of pious rascals who obviously manipulated others for their own benefit. On the contrary, the Book of Mormon witnesses suffered for their testimonies, receiving persecution in the Church—and after excommunication enduring ridicule and the great temptation to purge themselves of the scandal that their names continued to support. The Three Witnesses cut religious but not emotional ties with the Church, for they continued to identify with the Mormon people and regret their separation, no matter what their circumstances. In the end all had made the moral decision to finish life with their testimonies on their lips, two of them proclaiming their belief by the action of returning to the Church. History is not a tool for going far beyond external data. But it tells us what almost every interviewer said if he gave his impressions of the witnesses—that here were honest men stating what they obviously believed to be true. In short, no one who knows their lives well has claimed a conspiracy. They spoke too spontaneously of a moving experience when questioned by hundreds.

After history has done its job of portraying what the witnesses really were, the job of evaluating their testimony must be a matter of conscience. Conscience releases many souls lightly, but the greatest people have been sorely burdened by their inner light. "Necessity is laid upon me," exclaimed the apostle Paul. (1 Cor. 9:16.) The challenge of the witnesses is whether theirs was a God-given burden. Whatever it was, it operated in eleven different personalities throughout divergent lifetimes; they carried it through dramatic danger and the soft whisperings of self-interest. One may easily miss the real point. The question is not whether each agreed totally with Joseph Smith or the Church. Their commission was to speak firsthand of the Book of Mormon. If they did that convincingly while dissenting from other Mormon doctrines, their witness is really more, not less impressive. As the Three Witnesses left the Church, their brethren felt betrayed and bluntly labeled them, though no worse than Christ applying "Satan" to Peter voicing a materialistic gospel. (Matt. 16:23.) Peter and Jude in turn threw a dozen more scathing terms at the apostates of their day, for souls were at stake as they drew lines of authority clearly. One of these labels was the "way of Balaam" (2 Pet. 2:15; Jude 11), and Joseph Smith followed Jude's image to make William E. McLellin the false prophet Balaam and David Whitmer the dumb animal that he rode, since he was being used by McLellin.[2] This comparison has little to do with David Whitmer's honesty, but applies Jude's language to him as a rebel against God. This is an example of the anti-Mormon quotation being in reality a pro-Mormon argument, for LDS writers have long asked how Joseph Smith would dare to condemn the Book of Mormon witnesses if these men had the power to expose the Book of Mormon as a fraud. Joseph acts independently of them, as B. H. Roberts said, defying them to do their worst, dealing with them on the apparent assumption that their testimony was an eternal obligation.

The witnesses treat each other similarly, though each took an independent road. For instance, Oliver Cowdery died near

David Whitmer in upper Missouri in 1850, and nearly forty years later David said that in the previous year both men saw "that the Book of Doctrine and Covenants contained many doctrines of error."[3] In retrospect David claimed Oliver Cowdery to support his argument, but the documents from Oliver add other dimensions. Both obviously agreed in skepticism about polygamy, but Oliver Cowdery told the high council at Council Bluffs that he accepted the Nauvoo revelation taking presiding authority away from him and giving it to Hyrum Smith (D&C 124:94–95); afterwards Oliver supported the authority of the Twelve by expressing belief in the "calling of those men who have borne the burden since the death of Joseph."[4] At the end of 1849, when David said that they agreed totally, Oliver wrote a last letter accepting his Washington assignment from the Twelve and referring to them as "the good brethren of the valley."[5] David Whitmer gradually developed the position that there was no higher priesthood and no central presidency, but all of Oliver's returning speeches in 1848 emphasized that these offices and keys were given by angels in his presence.[6] So David is only partially right in claiming that he and Oliver agreed. It is naive to let David speak years later for Oliver when Oliver's contemporary language is now readily available. The point is that each witness separated himself from the others theologically after they separated themselves as a group from the Church. Their own lives and their own interests continued to evolve, but their impressive unity on their Book of Mormon witness remained intact.

The Three Witnesses were obviously affected in their doctrinal individualism by the number of years out of the Church. Oliver was absent a decade and could be expected to lack understanding on some important things revealed in his absence. This would be more true of Martin Harris after three decades before return, and intensified for David Whitmer after five decades without return. Time and human disillusionment were obviously working on their outlooks. Why not the same process of attrition for their Book of Mormon witness? When Mormonism was new, its young prophet had received a revelation promising the Three Witnesses "a view of the plates" and the ancient objects that accompanied them, with the command and prophecy: "And after that you have obtained faith, and have seen them with your eyes, you shall testify of them by the power of God, and this you shall do that my servant Joseph Smith, Jr., may not be destroyed, that I may bring about my righteous purposes unto the children of men in this work."[7] Each of the three quarreled with the Prophet's leadership, but scores of years later died after obedience to this 1829 command. Joseph Smith's prophecy was fulfilled in Oliver Cowdery in 1850, in Martin Harris in 1875, and not in David Whitmer until 1888. Time, geography, employment, and personality separated each witness from the others, but their diverging lives were fused by the fire of their testimonies into a sign for God that will continue to touch or to trouble thinking men.

The ultimate value of truth is that it needs no defense, only investigation. The words of the witnesses do speak for themselves, after analysis clears away garbled versions of what somebody attributed to them. All scriptures promise the Spirit's seal to those who sincerely hear, reflect, and pray. Joseph Smith and eleven more are modern witnesses of ancient scriptures; they are on God's errand to testify, as the above revelation commands, "that I may bring about my righteous purposes unto the children of men in this work." Their declarations concerning the Book of Mormon have been quoted extensively—both to show their historical consistency and to reveal their sincerity. Their words not only document events, but disclose their inner selves. If God indeed called them, their message carries the assuring peace of God.

Pope spoke of having "just enough of learning to mis-
quote." The Bible defender can be the offender, for in jealously
guarding his limited collection of prophets, he often opposes
more revelation with a few stock quotes that migrate from one
anti-Mormon book to another without much understanding
of the situation that produced them. The thoroughgoing ratio-
nalist sometimes seems open-minded by contrast. For
instance, the journalist Beardsley studied his subject enough
to realize that fraud was out of the question for the Three
Witnesses' testimony of the Book of Mormon: "But in this particular instance, they apparently spoke what they believed to
be the truth, when they asserted that they had seen the plates.
All three later apostatized . . . and during their periods of
apostasy were approached by numerous foes of the Mormons
and enterprising journalists who sought to obtain from them
statements refuting their testimony. All remained steadfast
until death in their assertion that they had seen the plates and
that they believed the Book of Mormon to be of divine origin."[8] But if the educated investigator better appreciates the
impact of the witnesses' testimony, his rationalism is often
threatened by miracles. He knows that the train is hurtling
down that track, and throws the switch to derail it from a
supernatural destination so foreign to a compact, scientific
world. But Beardsley's 1920 intellectual climate was more confident than a 1980 environment with so many questions still
unanswered. Then it seemed much easier to quote an early
psychologist who smugly spoke of these witnesses working
up their expectations to "a psychic mirage complete in every
detail."[9] Such rhetoric does not meet the central issue in Joseph
Smith's life. Fawn Brodie imitates Beardsley by expecting the
Three Witnesses to continue to bear testimony, since Joseph
"had conjured up a vision they would never forget." And how
is this done? Through "Joseph's unconscious but positive

talent at hypnosis."[10] Fine phrasing, but what does it mean? Those hypnotized are normally aware of entering such a process, and there were enough years apart from Joseph and from each other to reflect well on what had really happened. It may take more imagination to believe such theories about the witnesses than to accept their testimony.

One person is certain that there can be no more revelation after the Bible, and another is just as certain that there is no such thing as revelation. Both positions are essentially beyond logic, for neither assumption allows serious thought on the question of whether the Three Witnesses and Joseph Smith received revelation. Paul faced the same dilemma in preaching Christ when Jews rejected Jesus' resurrection because it was a "stumbling block" and rationalistic Greeks ridiculed it as "foolishness," or intellectually unrespectable. (1 Cor. 1:23.) But no one who arbitrarily limits his field of investigation can remain confident, because the possibility always exists that significant truth confronted him, and he looked the other way. Men as devout and as intelligent as any believer or skeptic today talked to the witnesses and concluded that they had indeed seen and heard. One of them was the brilliant Orson Pratt, whose logical report on the consistency of the Three Witnesses began this chapter. Another was the thoughtful dissenter John Corrill, who knew the witnesses intimately. He lost faith in the midst of the 1838 persecutions but explained why Mormonism touched him powerfully in the first place. His review of investigating the Book of Mormon witnesses suggests why their testimony must remain a lasting challenge to both Bible believer and skeptic: "As to the origin of the Book, I made every diligent inquiry, and from all I could learn, I became satisfied that Smith was the author, and I never have been able to trace it to any other source. As to its being a revelation from God, eleven persons besides Smith bore positive testimony of its truth. After getting acquainted with them, I was unable to impeach their testimony, and consequently thought that it was as consistent to give credit to them as credit the writings of the New Testament, when I had never seen the authors nor the original copy."[11]

What is at stake in the testimony of the Book of Mormon witnesses? A greater conception of the purposes of God, whose revelations reach beyond one area in the world and are not limited to antiquity. A Savior whose power extended to those seeking righteousness before he came upon earth, whose work today reaches out to every human soul, living or dead, ancient or modern. The unsurpassed sermon of all time puts the burden of decision upon every man: "for with what judgment you judge, you shall be judged." (Matt. 7:2.) The author of that sermon sent apostles, promising them that their experiences with him, his authority, and the Holy Spirit would equip them to be witnesses. (Acts 1:8.) To a sincere Roman their leader explained that the resurrected Jesus did not appear publicly, but to "witnesses chosen before of God." (Acts 10:41.) In early Acts the testimony of these apostolic witnesses is alive with inspiration and accountability, for they speak eloquently of God's light upon the humble and his judgment upon the proud. Nothing in religious history so parallels the actions of Joseph Smith, the men that gave their names to attest to new scripture, and new apostles called after them.

The fervent glow of the early Christian Church was kindled anew in the early meetings at the Whitmer home. As soon as the Book of Mormon could be published, the restored Church of Christ was organized April 6, 1830. Some thirty members and their interested friends gathered June 9 for their first conference, another Pentecost by the accounts of several who were there.[12] The record includes the first known reading of the initial Mormon doctrinal statement, then called the

189

"Articles and Covenants." (D&C 20.) Minutes also name ten Book of Mormon witnesses, who heard this revelation stress the Book of Mormon as "confirmed to others by the ministering of angels, and declared unto the world by them."[13] After these "Articles and Covenants" were "read by Joseph Smith, Jr.," they were "received by unanimous voice of the whole congregation, which consisted of most of the male members of the Church."[14] So the Book of Mormon witnesses personally endorsed this declaration of the eternal force of their testimony, grouped with other great miracles of gospel restoration: "Wherefore, having so great witnesses, by them shall the world be judged, even as many as shall hereafter receive this work, either to faith and righteousness, or to the hardness of heart in unbelief to their own condemnation. For the Lord God hath spoken it, for we, the elders of the Church, have heard and bear witness to the words of the glorious Majesty on high, to whom be glory forever and ever. Amen."[15]

NOTES

1. Journal of Discourses 18:159–161.

2. See Joseph Smith, Jr. to the Church, Dec. 16, 1838, Times and Seasons 1 (1840):83–84, cit. History of the Church 3:228. Cp. Numbers 22.

3. David Whitmer, An Address to Believers in the Book of Mormon (Richmond, Mo., 1887), p. 1.

4. Report to President Brigham Young by Orson Hyde, Apr. 5, 1849, manuscript written by clerk Robert Campbell.

5. Oliver Cowdery to Phineas Young, written after Aug., 1849, Richmond, Mo., cit. Stanley Gunn, Oliver Cowdery (Salt Lake City; Bookcraft, 1962), p. 261.

6. For background on Oliver's 1848 statements, see Richard Lloyd Anderson, "The Second Witness of Priesthood Restoration," Improvement Era, Sept. 1968, pp. 15 ff., and also "The Second Witness on Priesthood Succession," Improvement Era, Nov., 1968, pp. 14 ff.

7. D&C 17:3–4, first published in the 1835 edition as 42:2. Joseph Smith gave the date and circumstances in June, 1829 in HC 1:52–53. Cp. the 1831 manuscript evidence, ch. 1, n. 16: D&C 17:14, first published in the 1835 edition with the dating: "June, 1829, given previous to their viewing the plates containing the Book of Mormon." Early dissenter Ezra Booth saw a manuscript of this revelation in the summer of 1831: "When in Missouri, I had an opportunity to examine a commandment given to these witnesses, previous to their seeing the plates. They were informed that they should see and hear those

things by faith and then they should testify to the world." (Letter 3, [Ravenna] Ohio Star, Oct. 27, 1831.)

8. Harry M. Beardsley, Joseph Smith and His Mormon Empire (Boston:Houghton Mifflin Co., 1931), p. 67.

9. Ibid., p. 68.

10. Fawn M. Brodie, No Man Knows My History (New York: Alfred A. Knopf, 1946), pp. 77–78.

11. John Corrill, Brief History of the Church of Christ of Latter Day Saints (Saint Louis, 1839), p. 11. Cp. p. 16: "I have thus given a brief account of the investigation I went through in relation to these different subjects." At the end of the book Corrill speaks for "sound reason" by indicating that persecution had spoiled Joseph Smith's plans and prophecies. Like most prophets, Joseph had his plans deferred by persecution, but not destroyed. Corrill explains that he lost faith through 1838 events, not skepticism of the Book of Mormon witnesses, whom he knew intimately.

12. See especially HC 1:84–85.

13. Book of Commandments 24:11 (1833), printed there with the preface, "The Articles and Covenants of the Church of Christ," the same title of the two printings in The Evening and the Morning Star, June, 1832, and June, 1833, now D&C 20:10. Although there are minor modifications of D&C 20 for the verses used here, I have followed the first printings as being the closest known to the form of the revelation read on June 9, 1830.

14. Far West Record, June 9, 1830. Only priesthood holders appear by name, and this includes Joseph Smith and ten of the Book of Mormon witnesses. The unnamed witness, Jacob Whitmer, was undoubtedly there also, since the minutes list as present "most of the male members of the Church," and since he had been baptized April 11, 1830, according to HC 1:81.

15. Book of Commandments 24:12, the same text appearing in the 1832 and 1833 printings named in note 13 above, also cit. D&C 20:13–16.

Source Note

Behind every historical fact is a document, and responsible research relies on its most original available form. In this study these may be letters, journal entries, official minutes, newspaper stories, or later recollections. Most of the manuscripts quoted are found in the LDS Church Historical Department, Library and Archives Division. No note is made if a manuscript is held by the Historical Department, though location is indicated for documents at other libraries. Printed versions of manuscript sources are often given for the reader's convenience. In this case "cit." means that I have cited the printed source, though the more usual "also cit." means that I am quoting the original form and merely adding where the printed version may be found.

The present trend among Mormon historians is to quote documents very literally, including reproduction of misspellings. My practice is not to reproduce misspellings unless there is some special reason. Some documents are dictated, and some misspellings are accidental, but above all I feel an obligation as a researcher who has seen the original to relay it in readable form. Thus all quotations attempt to be exact copies of the manuscript source, with spelling occasionally modified, and punctuation and capitalization added. If there is any doubt on what is intended in spelling or meaning, that is noted.

The main printed source used in this work is Joseph Smith's history or autobiography, which he began to dictate in 1838 and which began to be published in installments in 1842 in the *Times and Seasons* as the "History of Joseph Smith." It was later reissued from 1902 on as Joseph Smith, *History of the Church of Jesus Christ of Latter-day Saints,* and is presently available in bound and paperback editions. My practice is to cite it as *History of the Church* at the first appearance in the chapter footnotes, with the abbreviation "HC" following. Another source frequently used is the history of Joseph Smith's mother, first published as Lucy Smith, *Biographical Sketches of Joseph Smith the Prophet and His Progenitors for Many Generations* (Liverpool, 1853), which is cited throughout as "*Biographical Sketches.*" Journal of Discourses is cited as Journal of Discourses at the first appearance in the chapter footnotes, with the abbreviation "JD" following. "JS-H 1" refers to the beginning of Joseph Smith's history in the new edition of the Pearl of Great Price. This account was previously referred to as Joseph Smith 2.

Appendix

Obtaining the Book of Mormon—
a Short Chronology

The following basic events come mainly from Joseph Smith's autobiography, with some help from his mother's history. Abbreviations are explained in the Source Note.

Date	Event	Source
Spring, 1820	Joseph Smith's first vision (revealing no church to be right)	HC 1:4-6 (JS-H 1:8-20)
September 21, 1823	Angel's first visit (announcing hidden plates)	HC 1:11-14 (JS-H 1:29-47)
September 22, 1823	Joseph's first view of plates (with angel's command to wait)	HC 1:14-16 (JS-H 1:48-53)
1823-27	Angelic teaching	HC 1:16 (JS-H 1:54)
January 18, 1827	Marriage of Joseph and Emma	HC 1:17 (JS-H 1:56-57)

Date	Event	Reference
September 22, 1827	Joseph receives the plates	HC 1:18 (JS-H 1:59–60)
September 23, 1827 (probably)	Joseph brings plates home (after hiding them)	*Biographical Sketches*, pp. 100–106
Fall, 1827	Martin Harris investigates (and gives Joseph $50 in aid)	HC 1:19 (JS-H 1:61)
December 1827	Joseph moves from Manchester, New York, to Harmony, Pennsylvania	HC 1:19 (JS-H 1:62)
February 27, 1828	Martin Harris takes transcript to New York City professors	HC 1:19–20 (JS-H 1:63–65)
About April 12 to June 14, 1828	Translation of first 116 manuscript pages (Martin Harris writing)	HC 1:20–21
Late June, 1828	Loss of 116 pages	HC 1:21, *Biographical Sketches*, pp. 117–22
Winter, 1828–29	Limited translation (with aid of family members)	HC 1:23–28; *Biographical Sketches*, pp. 124–26, 131
Winter, 1828–29	Teacher Oliver Cowdery boards with Joseph's parents (at Manchester, New York)	HC 1:32 (JS-H 1:66 *Biographical Sketches*, pp. 128–31

Date	Event	Reference
March, 1829	Prophecy of Three Witnesses (Martin Harris named)	HC 1:28–31 D&C 5
First week of April, 1829	Oliver Cowdery travels to Harmony, Pennsylvania	HC 1:32 (JS-H 1:66) *Biographical Sketches*, pp. 130–31
April 7 to June 1, 1829	Translation at Harmony, Pennsylvania (Oliver Cowdery writing)	HC 1:32–47 (JS-H 1:66–67)
May 15, 1829	Aaronic Priesthood restoration (by John the Baptist)	HC 1:39–43 (JS-H 1:68–75)
Late May, 1829 (probably)	Melchizedek Priesthood restoration (by Peter, James, and John) (JS-H 1:72);	Promise: HC 1:40 Fulfillment: D&C 27:12–13; Place: D&C 128:20
Early June, 1829	Move to Fayette, New York (with David Whitmer's aid)	HC 1:48–49
June, 1829 (probably)	Completion of translation at Whitmer home	HC 1:49–71
June 11, 1829	Copyright of Book of Mormon obtained	Book of Mormon, first edition, after title page
June, 1829	Promise of seeing plates to the Three Witnesses	HC 1:52–53 D&C 17

Date	Event	Reference
June, 1829	Three Witnesses see angel and plates, hear voice of God	HC 1:54–56 "Testimony" in Book of Mormon
June, 1829	Eight Witnesses see and handle plates	HC 1:57–58 "Testimony" in Book of Mormon
June–July, 1829	Negotiations for printing	See R. L. Anderson, "Gold Plates and Printer's Ink," *Ensign*, Sept., 1976, p. 75
August 25, 1829	Martin Harris mortgage to printer Egbert Grandin (for $3,000 printing cost)	Wayne County, N.Y. Land Records, Mortgages, book 3, p. 325
Fall–winter, 1829–30	Book of Mormon printing	HC 1:71–75, *Biographical Sketches*, pp. 142–51, Anderson, *Ensign*, Sept. 1976, pp. 75–76
March 26,1830	Book of Mormon offered for sale	*Wayne Sentinel* (Palmyra, N.Y.), Mar. 26, 1830
April 6, 1830	Organization of Christ's restored church	HC 1:75–80

Index

Anthon, Charles, visit of Martin Harris to, 6

anti-Mormon literature: unreliable methods of, 151, 166

Articles and Covenants, received by unanimous vote, 190, 191 n. 14

Beardsley, Harry, use of empty box story, 160

box, empty, story of convincing of witnesses, 159–61

Book of Mormon, Katharine Smith's testimony of, 26

breastplate, seen by Lucy Mack Smith, 24

Breslin, John, private investment of state funds by, 45

Brodie, Fawn: use of thirdhand information by, 152–53; use of empty box story, 160–61; hypnosis theory of, 187–88

Burgess, Harrison, a witness to the Book of Mormon, 162

Burnett, Stephen: account of Martin Harris's speech on plates, 155–56; differences with Church, 175 n. 9

Child, Jacob, defense of David Whitmer, 73–74, 75

Church of Christ, 70

conference, Church's first, 189–90, 191 n. 14

"Confession of Oliver Overstreet, A," 60–61

Corrill, John, investigation of Book of Mormon, 188–89, 191 n. 11

courtroom testimony of Oliver Cowdery, 57–60

Cowdery, Elizabeth Whitmer, confirmed Oliver Cowdery's testimony, 63

Cowdery, Oliver: priesthood restoration, 7; conversion of, 7; as scribe, 7, 28; as assistant president, 37–38, 47 n. 1; characterized by brother-in-law, 38; sided with Whitmers in land promotion, 38; resignation from Church, 38, 64 n.

201